Haunted by Waters

Haunted by Waters

Fly Fishing in North American Literature

Mark Browning

OHIO UNIVERSITY PRESS

Athens

Ohio University Press, Athens, Ohio 45701
© 1998 by Mark Browning
Printed in the United States of America
All rights reserved

Ohio University Press books are printed on acid-free paper ⊗ ™

05 04 03 02 01 00 99 98   5 4 3 2 1

Library of Congress Cataloging-in-Publication Data

Browning, Mark, 1962–
    Haunted by waters : fly fishing i North American literature /
Mark Browning.
        p.   cm.
    Includes bibliographical references and index.
    isbn 0-8214-1218-3 (alk. paper). — isbn 0-8214-1219-1 (paper :
alk. paper)
        1. American literature—History and criticism. 2. Fly fishing in
literature. 3. Canadian literature—History and criticism.
4. Fishing stories—History and criticism. 5. Masculinity
(Psychology) in literature. 6. Men in literature. 7. Fly fishing.
I. Title.
ps169.f56b76   1998
810.9'355—dc21   97-35279
                        cip

For two T.L.s and
my other small fry

Contents

Haunted by Waters

I

The View from Midstream

NEARLY 30,000 years ago, during the Magdalenian period, primitive humans depicted their hunting activities on the walls of Spanish and French caves, bequeathing to their distant descendants the earliest surviving human art. These paintings have been interpreted by archaeologists to be magic figures designed to ensure a successful hunt. Although the paintings typically represent land animals, they also include occasional depictions of fish, mostly trout and salmon (Sahrhage and Lundbeck 1992, 8). The subject matter of these paintings seems natural; what should loom more important in the lives of these artists than their means for feeding themselves? However, there is more significance to be drawn from the subjects of this first human art than the concerns of food and sustenance. For the primitive human, the act of hunting marks a boundary region between the role of the species as an equal member in the food chain and its eventual dominance of the ecosystem.

Many of the attributes that are said to distinguish humans from other animals can be found either directly or by inference on the walls of those European caves. Perhaps most obviously, humans are said to be tool-making and -using animals. Without the aid of spears and other weapons the primitive hunter would have little chance of felling the bison and bear pictured in the cave paintings. Humans are also said to be distinguished from animals by their use of language. A lone hunter would have little hope of success against the faster, larger, and stronger prey, but groups, co-operating and using language, were able to prevail. Humans are also said to be the only animals capable of rational thought, another attribute that served to equalize the struggle between those early hunters and their prey.

The precursors of *Homo sapiens* dwelled in forests and scavenged small prey. Fishing, according to Dietrich Sahrhage and Johannes Lundbeck, "developed gradually when man moved from the unselective and un-planned collection of things found in nature to the first systematic utiliza-tion of food, applying experience and newly invented simple techniques to the preparation of artifacts" (1992, 5). Biologists mark the emergence of these hominids from the forests to their pursuit of larger game on the sa-vannahs as the line of demarcation for the first *Homo sapiens*. This emer-gence might be called the transition from predation to hunting and from animal to human.

In addition to all the practical attributes described above, another fea-ture that distinguishes humans from all other animals is the propensity of humans to artistic expression. The cave paintings of France and Spain represent the earliest discovered human art, but little imagination is re-quired to reclaim the oral tales, long forgotten, that must have been told around the campfires of these hunters. It is quite plausible, then, that the earliest verbal art, as well as the earliest visual art, centered on the hunt. If the myths of pre-Columbian Native Americans and other "primitive" peoples are an accurate indication, these earliest literary creations proba-bly included not only tales of the exploits of the hunt but also myths ex-plaining the origins of various creatures and other natural phenomena.

The move from art depicting the hunt to that which we would call myth represents perhaps the most significant of all the human distinguishing attributes, self-awareness. The recorded myth structures and literatures of virtually all human cultures document a preoccupation with understanding that self—alone, in relation to others, and in relation to the natural (and sometimes supernatural) world. Literature, as a direct descendant of the human compulsion toward both artistic expression and myth, can be viewed as an investigation into what it means to be a human being, and that literature surrounding hunting (and its allied pursuit, fishing) occupies a unique boundary territory in this investigation, for, as described above, it takes for its subject the evolutionary steps that made modern humanity possible. The literature of the hunt can be viewed as the modern equivalent of a creation myth, meditating on the hazy area between being and nonbeing.

Although outdoor sports have generated a considerable literature, far more than half of that writing is centered not on the land, but on the aquatic hunt, fishing. When one considers the population of anglers compared with the population of hunters, fishing still seems to have enjoyed a disproportionate amount of coverage in the existing literature. In light of this fact, it is interesting to note that one current strand of evolutionary thought theorizes that humans did not come from the forests and onto the savannahs, as has long been believed. Instead, these biologists suggest, there was an intermediate step between the forest and the savannah during which humans were semi-aquatic, feeding on fish in shallow water. To these scientists, these semi-aquatic hominids represent the true beginnings of *Homo sapiens* as a distinct species. How fitting, then, if this theory is true, that humans in modern times seem drawn so readily to water, which Izaak Walton's Piscator calls "the eldest daughter of the Creation, the Element upon which the Spirit of God did first move, the Element which God commanded to bring forth living creatures abundantly; and without which those that inhabit the Land, even all creatures that have breath in their nostrils must suddenly return to putrefaction" (1993, 18), and more significantly drawn to the pursuit of fish.

According to Herbert Hoover, the thirty-first president of the United

States, "More people have gone fishing over more centuries than for any other human recreation" (1963, 28). Statistics would bear this claim out. According to the 1994 *Statistical Abstract of the United States*, as a recreational pursuit, fishing is practiced by nearly 20 percent of the population of the United States. A total of 30.6 million anglers bought 37.4 million fishing licenses in 1992; only 15.7 million hunters bought licenses in the same period. (The discrepancy in the numbers results from individuals who bought licenses for multiple states and for those who purchased special permits, such as trout stamps.) At a time when sales of hunting permits have remained relatively flat (15.4 million in 1970), fishing permit sales have steadily increased, rising by more than 25 percent between 1970 and 1992 (255). In 1992, those anglers spent an estimated 16,268,000 visitor-days fishing in national forests (250) and 511,000,000 fishing days on all waters in 1991 (255), averaging over fourteen days on the water per angler. Fishing equipment of all types accounted for sales of $9.3 billion, or $263 per person in 1992 (255). These anglers are male by a nearly two-to-one margin (258), and 87 percent of the purchases mentioned above were made by males (259). These numbers, while showing the magnitude in the aggregate of fishing in the United States, only begin to illustrate how broadly this avocation touches on Americans.

While fishing remains a male-dominated pursuit, it cuts across many other strata of society. Anglers of all ages participate in nearly equal proportions (14, 258). And, with the exception of the poorest census category, there is an even stronger correlation between percentage of households in a particular income group and the percentage of anglers from that income group (464, 258). Hoover states the situation simply: "The human animal originally came from out-of-doors. When spring begins to move in his bones, he just must get out again" (1963, 17).

Just as fishing as a sport seems to hold a remarkable fascination for Americans, it similarly seems to hold a disproportionate place in the literature of North America. Melville relates perhaps the greatest fishing story of all time in *Moby Dick*. Twain centers his greatest works on the greatest of American rivers. Hemingway returns several times to the subject of fishing. Moving from the traditional canon, one sees an enormous body of fishing literature, especially concerning fly fishing. From the earliest works in Britain, Dame Juliana Berners's early-fifteenth-century *Treatise of Fishing with an Angle* and Izaak Walton's *Compleat Angler* (1653), the researcher finds an unbroken stream of first British and then North American titles concerning the sport. William Humphrey remarks on the wealth of this tradition in his fiction:

> I sought instruction in books—no other sport has spawned so many. The literature of angling falls into two genres: the instructional and the devotional. The former is written by fishermen who write, the latter by writers who fish. I had read extensively in piscatorial prose of the devotional sort, searching always for the works of literature that some critics said were to be found there. I found one—if, that is to say, *Moby Dick* is a fish story. (1978, 52)

The depth of this literary resource is explained by one commentator: "fishermen read a great deal, and some of their cherished works would have received stock rejection slips if produced about any other subject. Fishing writers deal with a rather small corner of the world's works, and probably aren't being followed by Pulitzer scouts" (Chatham 1988, 119). In the introduction to a collection of writing about fly fishing, Leonard Wright adopts an apologetic tone for the apparent narrowness of his subject matter:

> To limit a collection of stories and articles to those about fishing with an artificial fly may appear, at first glance, to be cutting a very thin slice out of sporting literature. On closer examination, however, I think you'll find the opposite to be true. Fishing has produced a library that dwarfs that of any other sport, and the fly-fishing sections of these shelves contain the vast majority of quality books. (1990, 11)

It is to be expected that any activity that occupies the time of twenty percent of a large nation would produce a large bibliography, but as one moves closer to the subject this expectation begins to break down. While one in five of Americans is an angler, perhaps only one-fourth of those is a fly fisherman, yet the bibliography of fishing is skewed in exactly the opposite way. There is an enormous publishing record of books on trout, salmon, and other traditional concerns of fly fishing. There are relatively few written on the species and methods that are much more widely pursued. There are relatively few titles on black bass, for example, and nearly all of those are concerned with the practical aspects of the sport. There are virtually no book-length works on bream, crappie, and catfish.

Leaving the topic of fishing for a moment, one might argue that there is simply a great deal published on all topics, yet a search suggests that fly fishing holds a peculiarly privileged position. Millions enjoy such diversions as golf, baseball, and guitar playing, yet none of these pursuits boasts the extensive bibliography of fly fishing, which has fewer participants. If the search is narrowed to exclude technical and nonfiction works, the difference in the number of titles on the bibliographies grows wider. Clearly, fishing, and fly fishing in particular, occupies a position of peculiar importance in this culture. This position might be argued to descend from the cave painter and his existence in the boundary area of the species, yet the modern angler seems to bear little resemblance to this possible ancestor, and the modern fly fisherman, outfitted with graphite rod, neoprene waders, and finely tied flies seems more distant still. Nevertheless, the fly fisherman holds his position against the various currents.

Various writers have attempted to explain the human attraction to water. "We may, as some university biologists have argued, harbor a buried affinity for open grasslands, the remnant of some racial memory of our savannah-wandering ancestors. But water is a more ancient and elemental kind of genetic beacon. Though named for a whale, *Moby Dick* is a book about water" (Leeson 1994, 117). The same basic idea is presented by Jack Curtis, who suggests that "we cannot sanely escape, yet, from our ancestral water, and our mythology agrees with our physiology. Noah sails us out of the Flood; our urine is the same chemistry as brine" (Chatham 1988, 47).

Fishing might be said to represent humans at the threshold of humanity, but that representation is, if valid at all, only a distant genetic memory. More significantly to the angler of the twentieth century, fishing—and fly fishing in particular—represents, in a variety of ways, humans straddling a border region.

HIP deep in a Montana river, the North American fly fisherman of the twentieth century is an excellent representative of the American search for meaning. He—and it is overwhelmingly a he—is a divided person. He literally stands on the boundary between two worlds, the aquatic and the terrestrial, half submerged. This minor paradox bespeaks an array of other paradoxes in the fly fisherman. He often seems simultaneously to embody emotions of joy and melancholy. His success depends on nearly simultaneous action and repose. His sport requires a nearly scientific level of knowledge, yet at the same time requires an act of faith that a fish will rise. He is at once the enemy and the friend of the fish. His wise-use ethic (or frequently his catch-and-release methodology) makes him both captor and liberator. Bryn Hammond, in his wide-ranging sociological study of trout fishing and fishermen, captures a number of these paradoxes in one passage:

> The bond, as it were, between fisherman and fish must be water itself. But not merely the bond; the ineffable separation, too; that which forever keeps both apart. Maybe the sadness that almost always accompanies the angler's killing of a fish is something like this, and never resolved. The angler—the real angler, at least—strives to know the fish he seeks; but the only way he knows how to approach this desired end is to drag them up from their natural element into his own. That this often ends in the death of the fish that gives the angler such delight is, indeed, something of a paradox and a mystery. Catch and release is in part an act of conservation; a deliberate attempt by some anglers not to heedlessly destroy the objects of their hunting by water. It is also an act of the same assertiveness that drives the fisherman to fish in the same place, but without the mindless slaughter.
>
> The magic thread that binds angler to fish is the water itself, not just the fisherman's deceitful line and hook. Someone has said that if there is magic on this planet, it is contained in water. Water reaches everywhere; it touches the past and prepares the future. Aldo Leopold wrote, "The good life on any river may depend on the perception of its music, and the preservation of some music to perceive." (1994, 232)

Just as significant as this list of paradoxes is the position at which the fly fisherman stands. One might be first inclined to look upstream. Just as we might literally find him near the junction of cold mountain streams, the fisherman stands figuratively at the junction of several streams of tradition. One such stream is that flowing from the fishing tradition of the English gentleman, typified most prominently by Walton and preserved into the twentieth century by Frederic Halford. At several upstream points, springs bring the Judeo-Christian tradition into the flow. From the North American side of the watershed, the angler's river is fed by a trickle from the Native American tradition, and a major tributary from the Transcendentalist tradition. Also contributing to the water stalked by contemporary North American anglers is the long tradition of nature writing, and other, more recent tributaries.

As fascinating as the view upstream is, there is an equally compelling one downstream, and just as the upstream course is a divided one, so is that below. The fly fisherman, looking downstream, might find that this is the course that implies destiny. Like the heroes of many of the greatest American novels, the fly fisherman sets out, as Matthew Arnold categorizes people, seeking to *have* something (the trout) and in the end realizes that the more worthy goal is to *be* something. This distinction is one of the most significant dividing North American from British writers. The British fisherman seems to be much more like the one lampooned by Byron: "They may talk about the beauties of Nature, but the angler merely thinks about his dish of fish; he has no leisure to take his eyes from off the streams, and a single bite is worth to him more than all the scenery around" (*Don Juan*, canto 13, note). The North American is much more likely to speak of that very scenery that Byron accuses the British angler of ignoring. In fact, with this attribute in mind, it is very often possible to guess correctly the origin of a writer. For me the most difficult writer to categorize thus would be Roderick Haig-Brown, who was born in England and emigrated to Canada in early adulthood.

Another downstream view that the fisherman, in midstream, might study carefully is a larger one, that of the greater destiny of the ecosystem and the society. American outdoor writers have led the way to a wise-use ethic. Despite the significantly greater opportunity for fishing in North America than in the British Isles, it is in the United States that the practice of catch-and-release is observed at a nearly religious level, while in Britain the practice is still relatively rare. As noted above, the fly fisherman finds himself in the paradoxical position of saving a resource by consuming (or at least using) it. There is definitely an internal conflict between the desires to consume and to conserve.

While upstream and downstream hold our interest, fly-fishing literature in general focuses on the immediate, the here and now. In the here and now, various forces—physical, mental, spiritual, and emotional—tug and prod the representative angler. Certainly there are the physical forces of swirling waters and winds, but interesting are the internal challenges and struggles that give so much of this literature its raison d'être. American literature in general has often represented a double-minded struggle between disparate forces in a way distinct from the traditional sense of literary conflict. In earlier years, the prevailing struggle was between civilization and wilderness. Hawthorne, while appreciating the benefits of civilization, looked with a certain fascination as the wilderness retreated. Thoreau, on the other hand, embraced the wilderness, but could not wholly give up the benefits of civilization. In more recent years the struggle might be described as between individual and group. In such a category one might place Hemingway, with Nick Adams attempting to reconcile his broken individuality with the need to function in a society of others, some of whom were responsible for the physical and psychic wounding he experienced.

Currently, the wilderness-civilization conflict has taken on a new aspect, as Americans are no longer seen as heroic figures carving out a society in a vast wilderness, but as willful or ignorant barbarians, slowly destroying the small amount of remaining wilderness. In such an environment, the fly fisherman, far from the conqueror of nature, as he might have been presented in previous times, is instead portrayed as a savior, paradoxically dedicated to preservation because of his desire to consume.

The fly fisherman standing at midstream is far removed from his distant hunting or fishing ancestor who blazoned portrayals of the hunt on the walls of those caves, yet he still feels driven to acts of creativity that reflect his acts of consumption. Perhaps this is because, like the Neolithic precursor, modern humans attempt to represent in these works of art an understanding of the boundaries between human and animal, life and death, creation and destruction, beginning and end. All these enormous themes find a common connection at the end of a tapered line.

Although stopping short of the metaphysical level that he will eventually visit, Ted Leeson describes a complex web of connections involved with fishing, which has its point of origin at the simple dry fly:

> As both commencement and terminus, as the point of departure and culmination, the trout fly is the nexus of the sport, a tiny point from which radiate a thousand strands of our engagement. Despite its reliance on the line, fly fishing is not linear. It is radial and weblike. At the center is a rising trout, and millimeters above its nose is the fly. From it, paths trace outward to the engineering and art of tackle making, to geology and hydrology, botany and birds, aquatic and terrestrial insects, landscapes, books, history, photography, and a thousand other intersecting filaments that lead just as far as you wish to go. (1994, 49)

If one is to accept Leeson's description, fly fishing, and the fly most especially, is a sort of exceptional connecting point. Those who write of fishing, and fly fishing in particular, seek not simply to describe a sporting activity but to inscribe that web of connectedness in a more tangible and enduring form than casting will permit. These writers attempt to express the subtlety and complexity of human existence. An early American contributor to the literature of fly fishing expresses this sense of mystery and complexity in a 1927 essay:

> The mystery of fly-fishing, after all, is what is called by the younger generation a "complex." One of its strands—not the subtlest—is mere joy in manual dexterity. Another is the exquisite artificiality with which the means are adapted to the end. There is the pleasure of accurate observation of bewildering living creatures. There is moving water, and all the changes of the sky, shadow and sunlight and raindrops upon trees and flowers, and the old, inexhaustible, indescribable beauty of the world. There are a few fish. There is at times the zest of companionship and at other times the satisfaction of solitude. There are gentle memories of some "excellent angler, now

with God." And always there is that deep secret of expectation, the vital energy, ever strangely renewed, which looks for some fulfillment of its dreams beyond the next height of land, below the next turn of the stream. There are no scales for weighing such imponderable things as these, but surely next to the happiness of one's own home and work is the happiness of sitting in the bow of a canoe, rod in hand, as the guide paddles you noiselessly around the bend of an unknown river. Life offers few moments more thrilling than that, and one may be permitted to think that Death will not offer anything very different. (Perry 1927, 59–60)

One might wonder at the motivation of the fisherman who wades into the cold water of a trout stream. There are certainly less physically challenging ways in which one might spend an early spring morning, yet millions of anglers brave the elements each season and thousands of fly fishers drive to distant and dwindling fisheries in order to explore the mysterious web described above. Paradoxically, though, it is not simply the complexity that draws the angler. At the same time that the fly fisherman begins to challenge the uncertainty of his avocation, he will, in the best of times, find a sense of peace and certainty. Ted Leeson describes this sense well:

Every life has its points of fixity, certain small stillnesses in the incessancy of the world that anchor us with a sense of continuity and location. They are points of vantage and reference, places to stand from which the patterns of the past might be read and those of the future, perhaps, dimly inferred. For whatever reason, by karma or coincidence, such points in my own life have always centered upon rivers and streams and, above all, upon fly fishing for trout. Trout streams tug at the mind with an insistent, contradictory pull, presenting both a plain and perfect simplicity and a subtle link to sources of hidden significance; fundamentally alike, yet endlessly variable, they offer the solace of the familiar and the inexhaustible fascination of a thing that can never fully be known. (1994, 1–2)

Such discussion is reminiscent of T. S. Eliot's opening lines of "Burnt Norton," in which he seeks for the still place at the center of the circle, and it is here that one finds the final paradox of the fly fisherman. Although his place in midstream can be described in terms of divisions, conflictedness, and border tension, the literature suggests that through this very brokenness, the successful angler finds wholeness.

AS the modern fly fisherman (or woman) succumbs to the dying light of evening and steps out of the water for the day, there is a sense that something more has been accomplished than simply netting a half dozen rainbow trout and carefully releasing them back to the deep, cold waters of a favorite pool. There is a sense that connections have been made, between "time present and time past," to return to Eliot, between divided aspects of the self, or perhaps between human and nature. There is, above all, a sense of something larger than just the pursuit of fish. Similarly, in studying the literature of fly fishing, it becomes clear that something more has been accomplished.

If, as some posit, fly fishing is a metaphor for life, then it might be suggested that fly fishing literature is a metaphor (or archetype) for literature in general, with North American fly-fishing literature giving the reader a unique view into the distinctive but difficult-to-define field of American literature. This is, perhaps, an overreaching idea, but fishing depends on the hope that some leviathan lunker is lurking behind the next rock or at the base of the next undercut bank. For the fisherman, such a hope is essential and overwhelming, virtually forcing the next cast, until failing light or some other necessity forces him from the water; for the reader, too, the hope of one last and lasting connection is enough to sustain one more page, one more chapter, one more book, ad infinitum. With each cast among the pages, there is the hope that a connection will be made in these dark and difficult waters, a connection that will bring all the others, past and future, into order, a connection that will carry the reader-angler back to the very origins of the species.

Though many have tried to express this idea, Norman Maclean, at the end of *A River Runs through It,* conveys it best:

> Eventually, all things merge into one, and a river runs through it. The river was cut by the world's great flood and runs over rocks from the basement of time. On some of the rocks are timeless raindrops. Under the rocks are the words, and some of the words are theirs.
>
> I am haunted by waters. (1976, 104)

What follows is not an attempt to exorcise Maclean's water spirits, but to better enjoy the haunting.

Interlude 1

The Frog

ONE *of my earliest memories revolves around fishing—not around me fishing, but my dad. I was probably four years old when my father went on a fishing trip with a couple of friends to Great Bear Lake, a place that I have since found to be located far north, in the western reaches of Canada. I don't know for sure why that memory sticks in my mind for his absence was not all that remarkable in those days. I don't think that the memory has to be traced to the time after the trip when I saw photographs of my father, clad in a strange hat and plaid mackinaw, holding a monstrous muskie up for the camera. He wore a faint smile in those pictures, the same smile you'll see on his face in the few pictures where he can be found holding me. It was, unless I miss my guess, a smile of a self-made, very successful bank president who suddenly found himself holding a creature that he wasn't entirely comfortable with, the smile of a man forty-five years of* age finding himself holding not his first grandson, but third son. Or maybe it was just the smile of a proud man who really wanted to get in out of the Arctic wind. I hate to be too presumptuous.

While the Great Bear memories are basically those of absence, another entire set of memories can be found just a few years later, when I discovered my father's tackle box. It was a modest-sized metal thing, created in the days before Plano was filling Kmart with cheap, plastic tackle boxes, that open in three places, exposing a terrific cascade of shelves and boxes. This was a simple box, sporting two shelves and tinged with rust in a couple of places. Inside, it bore a faint musty smell that I couldn't quite place, but it seemed all the more exotic and exciting for the odor.

I can't be sure whether I was actually supposed to have access to this little treasure chest or not. I rather think that my mother would have been mortified at the thought of me and all those rusty, dirty fishhooks in one place, so probably I stole surreptitious looks at the angling bounty my father had amassed over the years in quiet sojourns in the utility room.

That tackle box, while it held many wonders wrought in balsa wood and with treble hooks dangling from every conceivable point, contained one object that was so wonderful, so utterly captivating, that its image remains etched boldly across my mind even today. It was the frog.

No jig or plug could begin to compare with the frog. In hindsight, the frog was probably a catastrophe as a fishing lure. The fact that you can't buy one today testifies rather strongly to that, but to a six-year-old eye, this creation was the most remarkable thing possible to behold. Cast in mildly flexible plastic, the frog looked remarkably like a real frog. A wire eye protruded from its mouth through which the angler could tie the line and a single, rather huge hook. These features and the admirably convincing paint job on the frog's back might have been wonderful enough, but the frog's greatest claim to preadolescent fascination was in its legs.

I had probably played with the frog half a dozen times before I realized his greatest ability, which was that if one pulled on the eye in his mouth, his legs extended from their normal bent position to an outstretched, jumping position. Apparently, the designer's idea was that while an angler navigated the frog through likely looking bass territory, a few sharp tugs on the line would send the frog into such a realistic simulation of frog swimming that no bass in the world would be able to resist a quick meal. Forget that the lure possessed such a girth that only the largest bass would have the nerve to attack, or that the swimming mechanism required such titanic tugs that anyone who managed to actually get the legs working would pull the lure through the water so fast that no self-respecting fish would have anything to do with it. These minor drawbacks never entered my mind in those days. The first drawback, in fact, I saw as a strong-point, for in those days, as any kid I ever fished with knew, you always tied on the largest lure you could get your hands on because you wanted to catch the biggest fish in the lake. And as I think back on it, there was probably a six-inch bluegill in the Lake of the Ozarks that would have tried to take the frog in a single gulp. You've got to love bluegills, but that's another story.

At about the same time that I discovered the frog, our family bought a cabin at the Lake of the Ozarks. I remember bouncing down to the dock, toting the three-foot rod that my sister's husband had brought me from his store. This was my first fishing expedition, although to call fishing off the dock an expedition might be a trifle grandiose.

Regardless of what the morning was to be called, I knew what lure I wanted at the end of my line. With my dad busy doing something nearby, I rifled through the tackle box—I had by now memorized the location of every item—and quickly laid my hands on the frog.

"Tie this on for me, Dad!" I urged, knowing that he would be impressed with my wisdom in lure selection.

He glanced over his shoulder at me. "You can't fish with that thing."

He was, of course, wrong. You can tie a 1957 Buick to your line and drag it around the water if you want to. What he meant and what he should have told me was that I'd never in a million years catch anything with the frog. That would not have dissuaded me, but it is what he should have said.

"Yeah, I can!" I shot back.

He sighed and shook his head a bit. "It's too big," he finally offered. From the look in his eye, I think he knew what I was going to say next.

"But I want a big lure so I can catch big fish!"

It's not often that my dad doesn't know what to say. I've long been impressed with the fact that he is almost always capable of a response and that his responses are almost never unreasoned or irrelevant, but this day he stood speechless for a minute or so before relenting. "Tell you what," he said. "I'm going to give you something special."

"But I want the frog!"

"You can have the frog," he said. "And anything else you want, because I'm going to tie you on"—he rummaged around in the box for a moment—"a swivel!"

I looked at what appeared to be a deformed brass safety pin and watched as my dad tied it to my line.

"All you have to do is open it here and you can put the frog or anything else on your line," he said as he pulled his knot tight.

I think I fished the frog hard for about ten minutes before switching to some other lure. By the time my mother yelled down that lunch was ready, I'd been through half the tackle box and hadn't even brushed up against a fish that I knew of. To my recollection, in our two years at that lake cabin, I never caught a fish. In the years that we spent at our second lake house, I caught a lot of fish, although sadly the frog was lost on some underwater snag and presumably rests even today beneath thirty feet of brown water.

I'm thirty-four years old as I write these words. Like my father, I have four children. In three months, my father will be eighty. Although he's taught me many things, he didn't teach me to fly cast, nor did he pass his tackle box on to me or either of my brothers. In fact, in the thirty-four years we have shared on this earth, I don't believe that my father and I have ever caught a fish together. Perhaps that's a shortcoming we should remedy.

2

Upstream: The European Fork

WHILE the ideal of the United States as a melting pot has perhaps been oversold, it is no exaggeration to describe the North American fly fisher as an amalgam of numerous traditions or, as presented previously, standing below the confluence of a number of streams of tradition. Before proceeding to examine the resulting river, it seems appropriate to study each of the tributaries in order to see what each brought to the watershed.

Biblical Roots

Whether overtly religiously oriented or not, all the European streams of thought leading to the formation of North American fly-fishing literature must be seen as reflecting the Judeo-Christian heritage represented in the texts of the Bible and those ancillary to them. A survey of this literature can be achieved by reviewing the fairly narrow portion of the biblical record in which fish or fishing figures prominently.

There are relatively few mentions of fish in biblical literature; the words *fish* or *fishes* appear forty-one times in one prominent concordance to the Old and New Testaments. By comparison, the same concordance lists 140 appearances of *sheep*, another prominent symbol in both Judaism and Christianity. With the exception of the book of Jonah, the significance of fish in the Old Testament is virtually nonexistent. In the animal imagery of the New Testament, however, that of fish is second only to sheep imagery in terms of frequency and significance.

Probably the best remembered reference to fishing and fishermen is found as Jesus calls two of his followers: "And Jesus, walking by the sea of Galilee, saw two brethren, Simon called Peter, and Andrew his brother, casting a net into the sea: for they were fishers. And he saith unto them, Follow me, and I will make you fishers of men." (Matthew 4:18–19). Norman Maclean begins *A River Runs through It* by describing his father's attitude toward these apostles: "He told us about Christ's disciples being fishermen, and we were left to assume, as my brother and I did, that all first-class fishermen on the Sea of Galilee were fly fishermen and that John, the favorite, was a dry-fly fisherman" (1). In truth, of course, Peter and Andrew not only failed to meet Maclean's expectation as fly fishermen, but were not even anglers in the sense of using a hook, line, and rod, as the passage from Matthew describes the men casting a net into the sea. Later in the story of the gospels, the evangelists once again describe the fishermen fishing with a net. In Luke, this event takes place early in the story, presumably at the same time that Matthew describes the calling. In this tale, Jesus is described as launching out from shore in a small boat owned by Peter. At an appropriate point, Jesus tells Peter to "launch out into the deep, and let down your nets for a draught" (Luke 5:4). Peter responds, indicating that although they had fished all night they had caught nothing. In casting the nets, though, they caught so many fish that the nets broke and the fish, somehow landed, threatened to sink the boats.

In John's gospel, the same essential story is placed after the resurrection, when Jesus appears to the disciples, who have inexplicably decided to go fishing. In this telling of the story, Jesus admonishes the disciples to "cast the net on the right side of the ship, and ye shall find" (John 21:6). In this case, again, the men are scarcely able to handle all the fish that they net, dragging 153 fish to shore, where they enjoy a meal with Jesus. One small portion of this story is saved for the last chapter of Luke's gospel, as Jesus appears to the disciples and asks for meat: "And they gave him a piece of a broiled fish, and of an honeycomb" (Luke 24:42). J. C. Fenton suggests that if "the catch of fish is a symbol of the evangelistic mission of the disciples, the meal seems to be in some sense a symbol of the Eucharist" (209).

One other prominent occurrence of fish in the gospels is in the story in which Jesus feeds a multitude with five loaves and two fishes. This story appears in all four gospels (Matthew 14:14–21; Mark 6:34–44; Luke 9:12–17; John 6:1–14) with a second telling appearing in two of the gospels, with seven loaves and a few fish (Matthew 15:32–38 and Mark 8:1–9). One common interpretation for this story is that no real miracle occurred in the sense of food being multiplied. Instead, William Barclay suggests in his commentary on John's account, "this story represents the biggest miracle of all—one which changed not loaves and fishes, but men and women" (204). This interpretation has its modern parallel in the stories that suggest that many anglers miss the point of fishing, assuming that it has something to do with the fish, when it really has everything to say about the anglers themselves.

Probably the strangest use of fish as a symbol in biblical texts is an occurrence in which Jesus is being questioned regarding his obligation to pay taxes. Employing what seems strangely like a parlor trick, Jesus instructs Peter, "[G]o thou to the sea, and cast an hook, and take up the fish that first cometh up; and when thou hast opened his mouth, thou shalt find a piece of money: that take, and give unto them for me and thee" (Matthew 17:27). The story does not indicate that Peter actually carries out this instruction; thus at least one commentator has suggested that Jesus is engaged in a use of hyperbole, essentially saying that Peter can go back to his job for a day and pay the tax that way (Barclay 1978, 172).

In attempting a synthesis of the use of fish and fishing in biblical literature, it will be noticed that virtually all the significant use of such imagery occurs in the four gospels. As noted above, with the exception of the book of Jonah, the Old Testament does not use fish in any meaningful way. Pauline and other New Testament texts include virtually nothing from this vein.

Fish are a mysterious quantity for the gospel writers, unlike sheep, which are easily observable and rather unsophisticated animals. Fish multiply to feed as many as might be needed. Fish mysteriously appear when none have been caught for many hours. Fish presumably might be found carrying coins about for the payment of taxes. Perhaps most significantly, though, fish are a metaphor for people, as Jesus implores the brothers to become fishers of men. Fishing, as seen from the biblical perspective, is not simply a way of feeding oneself, but of making connection with the ineffable. It is reaching into the unseen and drawing out life.

The English Tradition

The home waters of fly fishing are undeniably found in the Test River in England. The original contributor to the great tradition of British fishing literature is less certainly named. *The Treatyse of Fysshynge Wyth an Angle*, written in approximately 1450 and published in 1496 as part of the second *Book of St. Albans*, is widely attributed to a nun, Dame Juliana Berners, although just as widely that authorship is questioned. If Berners's authorship is not valid, it is understandable that she might have the *Treatise* assigned to her name. The first *Book of St. Albans*, a work on hunting, hawking, and heraldry, included a *Boke of Huntyng* specifically attributed to "Dam Julyans Barnes," the only explicitly named author in the volume. John McDonald calls this compilation in which Berners's earlier work appears "the most celebrated book on field sports in English, the first English sporting book to be printed, and one of the earliest English printed books, issued nine years after Caxton's first in England" (1963, 68).

One of the difficulties scholars have encountered in enthusiastically attributing the authorship of the *Treatise* to Berners is certainly misogyny, but another, more valid and difficult to escape, is the lack of continuity between the two works. In the *Book of Hunting*, Berners not only does not treat the subject of fishing, but she treats one of the subjects of the later fishing book, hunting, in a much different light. Far from being simple diversions for the upper class, the subjects of the first book were "fundamentals of a polite education and necessary for the competent discussion of literature as well as correct behavior" (McDonald 1963, 69). One must simply reflect on *Sir Gawain and the Green Knight* or Sir Thomas Malory to understand the truth of this statement.

Gawain and Arthur, however, do not go fishing, and while in the *Book of Hunting* Berners embraces hunting as a proper pursuit for a young man aspiring to knighthood, in the *Treatise of Fishing*, she dismisses hunting as

> too laborious. For the hunter must always run and follow his hounds, laboring and sweating very painfully. He blows on his horn till his lips blister; and when he thinks he is chasing a hare, very often it is a hedgehog. Thus he hunts and knows not what. He comes home in the evening rainbeaten, scratched, his clothes torn, wet-shod, all muddy, this hound lost and that one crippled. Such griefs happen to the hunter—and many others which for fear of the displeasure of them that love it, I dare not report. (1963b, 45)

Berners continues in the *Treatise of Fishing* similarly to criticize hawking and fowling, settling eventually on fishing, and specifically fishing with an "angle" or hook, as the most likely means to achieve a "merry spirit," which she set out to discover at the outset of the work, using as her epigram Proverbs 17:22, "*Animus gaudens aetatem floridam facit*," which is translated in the manuscript as "a glad spirit makes a flowering age—that is to say, a fair age and a long one" (1963a, 27). She suggests that three things contribute to the creation of this "glad spirit": merry thought, work that is not excessive, and a moderate diet. Clearly the Berners who extols fishing seems to differ greatly not only in subject matter but also in attitude from the Berners who wrote of hunting.

The point of this contrast, in the present context, is not to question Berners's authorship, but to illustrate that *The Treatise of Fishing with an*

Angle marks a significant shift in thought patterns that will be magnified in the coming years. If Berners is the author of both works, she, like the fly fisherman in midstream, stands in a boundary region, between the Middle Ages and Renaissance, reflecting the chivalrous ideal in the hunting book, while presenting the more reflective and populist ideal in the fishing book. R. B. Marston notes that the first book was published "a few months after the last battle of the War of the Roses" (1894, 10), and thus at the very close of the Medieval period. One might imagine that, having placed behind them the years of internecine war, fueled partly by the ideals represented in the chivalric code that the *Book of Hunting* exemplifies, Berners and her countrymen determined to pursue more relaxing sport and retired to the streamside. That is, of course, an oversimplification, but it is not overly simple to suggest that the *Treatise of Fishing* is more representative of the Tudor-Renaissance era then dawning in England, while the *Book of Hunting* hearkens back to the Plantagenet-Medieval era that was drawing to a close.

What Berners has to say about fishing is perhaps less remarkable than that she speaks of fishing at all. Unlike the outgoing pursuits of hunting and falconry, fishing offers a more conservative and introspective activity. There is little focus on what the angler has to gain from his pursuit, but rather a concern for the avoidance of bothers. "For he can lose at the most only a line or a hook. . . . So then his loss is not grievous, and other griefs he cannot have, except that some fish may break away after he has been caught on the hook, or else that he may catch nothing" (1963b, 46). With a limit to his losses, Berners suggests, the angler can focus on the possible joy of catching a fish. "And if the angler catches fish, surely then there is no man merrier than he is in his spirit" (46). But the joy of the catch is not the only area of reward that Berners delineates for the angler. She, for the first time, mentions the ancillary benefits to the angler:

> And yet, at the very least, he has his wholesome and merry walk at his
> ease, and a sweet breath of the sweet smell of the meadow flowers, that
> makes him hungry. He hears the melodious harmony of birds. He sees the
> young swans, herons, ducks, coots, and many other birds with their
> broods, which seems to me better than all the noise of hounds, the blasts

of horns, and the clamor of birds that hunters, falconers, and fowlers can produce. (46)

After her introductory passage proving angling to be the best means of achieving Solomon's ideal of a "glad spirit," Berners proceeds to more mundane matters, such as the crafting of fishing tackle, when and where to seek individual species, what flies to use, and related matters. She describes each species individually, noting that "the salmon is the most stately fish that any man can angle for in fresh water" (56) and calling the trout "a right dainty fish" (57).

In concluding the *Treatise*, Berners enjoins her readers to follow a few matters of etiquette, such as not fishing on private property without permission, and then proceeds with an admonition:

> Also, you must not use the aforesaid artful sport for covetousness, merely for the increasing or saving of your money, but mainly for your enjoyment and to procure the health of your body and, more especially, of your soul. For when you intend to go to your amusements in fishing, you will not want very many persons with you, who might hinder you in your pastime. And then you can serve God devoutly by earnestly saying your customary prayers. And in so doing, you will eschew and avoid many vices, such as idleness, which is the principal cause inciting a man to many other vices, as is right well known. Also, you must not be too greedy in catching your said game, as in taking too much at one time, a thing which can easily happen if you do in every point as this present treatise shows you. That could easily be the occasion of destroying your own sport and other men's also. (65–66)

Carl Otto von Kienbusch concurs with the division of the *Treatise of Fishing* into three parts: "The first sets forth the superiority of angling over other forms of sport, the second lists the items of an angler's equipment and gives instructions for their production and use against certain fishes, the third is devoted to the mental, ethical, and spiritual qualities found in the perfect angler." Von Kienbusch insists that, whoever the author of *The Treatise of Fishing with an Angle* might be, whether male or female, "these twenty-three pages set the pattern for hundreds of volumes that fill our shelves" (1958, 1).

Between Berners and the first appearance of Izaak Walton's *The Compleat Angler* in 1653, a steady flow of fishing literature tutored the English angler on how best to pursue his quarry. *The Art of Angling*, recently attributed to William Samuel (*Three Books on Fishing*, vii) appeared in 1577. Leonard Mascall's *Book of Fishing with Hook and Line*, largely plagiarized from Berners, was published in 1590. In 1600, John Taverner produced *Certaine Experiments Concerning Fish and Fruite,* a book more concerned with the husbandry of fish ponds than with angling. John Dennys, in 1613, published *Secrets of Angling,* a book in verse, which does not deal directly with fly fishing. British writer R. B. Marston notes that Dennys might not be Berners's equal in practical instruction but "he is far ahead of all other English angling writers who have attempted to describe the art in verse" (1894, 70). *The Pleasures of Princes*, by Gervase Markham, appeared in 1614, a popular book drawing heavily on Berners, Mascall, and Dennys. Finally, only two years before Walton's first edition, there appeared Thomas Barker's *The Art of Angling* in 1651.

The interrelations of these books, each one drawing on one or more of its predecessors, leads one bibliographer to the following: "The genealogy of English fishing books is long and complicated, but for most readers—as for most anglers—there is one ancestor which attracts all pious veneration" (Bentley 1958, 67). This one ancestor is, of course, Izaak Walton's *The Compleat Angler,* "that lovely bucolic idyll, the most famous book in all the literature of sport" (von Kienbusch 1958, 2), first published in 1653 with subsequent and expanded editions in 1655, 1661, 1668, and 1676. This last edition was the final one published during Walton's lifetime and the first to contain Charles Cotton's book on trout fishing. Walton, like his predecessors, draws on those who wrote before him. He openly cites Dennys, Markham, Barker, and Mascall, quoting directly from Dennys and Barker (Bentley 1958, 69). It is not in his similarity to his predecessors that Walton is remarkable, however. For while those before him had been largely practical and didactic, Walton brings a more creative quality to his text, which contains "a narrative which envelopes teaching in the delights of story and description" (Bentley 1958, 70). Using dialogue between two friends, Piscator and Viator, as his organizing principle, Walton introduced narrative, rich description, and a sense of drama to his work, interspersing little poems and songs into the text. The dialogue, which had long been thought to be Walton's unique creation, was discovered in the early 1950s to have been almost certainly borrowed from William Samuel's *The Arte of Angling* (1577), which not only employs a dialogue format but also uses Piscator and Viator as the names of his principals.

Having titled his great work *The Compleat Angler, or, The Contemplative Man's Recreation*, Walton might be assumed to be simply a happy soul who enjoyed fishing and possessed a literary bent, but his literary output began with biographies of Donne and Sir Henry Wotton. It was not lazy summer days that sent Walton streamside, but rather the ascendancy of Cromwell. With the execution of Charles I in 1649, Walton, a devout Anglican, found himself increasingly marginalized. While *The Compleat Angler* is certainly a book of instruction on fishing, it is at the same time a set of instructions for life, and a sort of coded message to Anglicans, with Anglers serving as a not-too-subtle metaphor for his fellow-believers (Bevan 1993, xviii). It is at this juncture that the book takes on greater significance for the present study and where its critics have often missed the point. One critic has noted that

> Walton has been canonized as the angler's saint, the source of knowledge where fishing is concerned. His elevation to this pinnacle has been achieved to a large extent by those who have not read his book. Walton added almost nothing to what was already known, his experience being limited. Bait fishing was his proper sphere. He never caught a salmon and what he learned about fly fishing was mostly at second hand. (von Kienbusch 1958, 2)

Richard Franck, a Cromwellian soldier, writing in 1658, similarly assails Walton's lack of new wisdom, noting that Walton "has imposed upon the world this monthly novelty [the twelve flies for trout, which derive from Berners's *Treatise*], which he understood not himself; but stuffs his book with morals from Dubravius and others, not giving us one precedent of his own practical experiments" (qtd. in Walton 218).

Where Berners begins to suggest that fishing is about more than just fishing, Walton does so openly. Bryn Hammond describes the post-Walton attitude as follows:

> By 1676 and the publication of Walton's 5th edition, coupled with Cotton's 1st edition as Part 2 of *The Complete Angler*, going fishing became more of an event once again, and the sentiment *Piscator non solum piscatur* (there is more to fishing than catching fish) became not only acceptable, but the prime reason for going fishing. In this respect Walton's influence was not only singular, but persists to this day and has permeated much of the vast literature on angling since that time. (4)

By making this move, Walton not only allows the reader to understand that there is far more to fishing than simply catching fish, but also uses his text as a sort of parable of his particular version of Christianity. Interestingly, as the early Christians used the sign of the ιχτηψσ to camouflage their activities, so does Walton some fifteen centuries later use fish to camouflage his Anglican spirituality.

Although Walton had undoubtedly passed into immortality with the success of *The Compleat Angler*, he was not without his detractors. In *A River Runs through It*, the Maclean brothers poke fun at Walton, noting, "The bastard doesn't even know how to spell 'complete'" (5). A somewhat more literary criticism came from Byron, who had little sympathy for Walton or for anglers in general, commenting in *Don Juan* on both the author and his followers:

> And angling, too, that solitary vice,
> Whatever Izaak Walton sings or says:
> The quaint, old, cruel coxcomb, in his gullet
> Should have a hook, and a small trout to pull it.

Byron continues his diatribe, claiming that the angler has no interest outside of his "dish of fish" and that he cannot take his eyes from the stream to appreciate that wonder that is around him. "But angling! No angler can be a good man" (qtd. in Hammond 1994, 161). That Byron remained of the minority party in regard to attitudes toward fishing cannot be questioned, yet, despite the rather offhand nature of his remarks, he does raise two points that can, with minimal overgeneralizing, be said to typify the British attitude toward angling, especially as it is contrasted with the attitude that has evolved in the twentieth century in North America—notably, whether the angler is cruel and whether the angler is single-mindedly fixed on the goal of catching fish.

A review of fishing literature published in the golden age of British angling, the Victorian and Edwardian periods, illustrates that while anglers in Walton's period might have truly subscribed to the *Piscator non solum piscatur* credo, those who came after either completely abandoned that ideal or relegated it so far behind the primary conflict between angler and fish that it disappears altogether from the literature. John William Dunne, one of the most significant British fishing writers of the early twentieth century, goes to great length in his first chapter to make the point that anglers stray when they become overly consumed with the task of exactly mimicking nature. Having early in his fishing been mystified at some of the contents of a selection of flies he had purchased, he realized one day while on the river that these flies were indeed the elusive "blue-winged olives" (1–12). There is, in Dunne, nothing like the introductory chapter that might be found in writers as far back as Berners and up to the present day, positioning angling in general or this trip in particular in a larger philosophical field. Gone is the scheme that served all angling writers from Berners to Walton, by which the first task that must be accomplished is to celebrate or validate angling as a worthy pursuit. Such a chapter, although very different in tone and content from what Berners and Markham have left, seems obligatory in American writings. An American contemporary of Dunne, Bliss Perry, whose *Pools and Ripples* was published in 1927, prefaces his collection of fishing articles with an explanatory note, justifying not only fishing as a sport but his own approach to it, which included fishing with worms.

There is nothing of the contemplative nature to be found in Dunne, however. In chapter two, he forges ahead very practically, discussing the manner in which one should compare colors: against the sky, as the fish might perceive the fly (13–24). For Dunne and the others whom he represents, fishing is not the "Contemplative Man's Recreation" as Walton would have it, but is instead a return to primitive existence and a form of warfare. According to Dunne, the "origin of that excitement [of success in hunting or fishing] may possibly be traced to the days when success or failure in these pursuits meant, to primitive man, all the stark difference between satiety and starvation" (101). He describes the difference between a game and a sport in the fact that in a game your opponent is another person, while in a sport your opponent is "Nature herself—Nature, wild and free and entirely lawless,—Nature, wayward, cheating, laughing, alluring, infinitely diversified, entrancingly mutable" (102).

At about the same time, in 1924, John Waller Hills was fishing the legendary rivers of England. In "The Iron Blue," Hills details a challenging day on England's Test River. The fishing is best described as a conquest. "A fish rose just where the quick run left the pool, on the very lip, and if ever I saw a fish between 3 and 4 pounds it was he. No fisherman could possibly leave such a prize" (1990, 38). He describes trying a couple of casts, changing flies, and finally drawing a rise out of the trout. "I reeled furiously, felt the fish, off he careered again, but my line brushed against something, underwater weed no doubt; only a touch, but it was enough, he was off. What a tragedy" (38). "Thus ended the day, a day of hard work, and of failure mingled with success. What more can the fisherman desire? And what sport can compare with fishing?" (41). There is a sense of dividedness in Hills's writing, yet more prevalent is the idea that the sport is a form of battle, in which the fish is to be first deceived, then captured, and finally devoured. Where many contemporary American writers would draw a highly introspective 1,500 words—or an entire novella, as in the case of William Humphrey's My Moby Dick—out of the mighty fish that got away, Hills describes the loss as a "tragedy."

At about the same time that Theodore Gordon was floating his first dry flies on the Beaverkill, Theodore Roosevelt, writing of hunting, pronounced a stern judgment against the British sporting tradition:

> To my mind this is one very unfortunate feature of what is otherwise the admirably sportsmanlike English spirit in these matters. The custom of

shooting great bags of deer, grouse, partridges, and pheasants, the keen rivalry in making such bags, and their publication in sporting journals, are symptoms of a spirit which is most unhealthy from every standpoint. (Roosevelt 1990, 291)

A final example of the single-mindedness of the mainstream of British fly-fishing writing can be found in Huish Edye, who, working in the 1940s, detailed how one might find and catch the largest trout in any stream. "The term 'good' as applied to trout is relative to the stock of any given water. A good fish is something considerably bigger than the merely adult trout—an exceptionally heavy trout" (1990, 183–84). This article is reminiscent of contemporary ones in American bass-fishing magazines, detailing the how-tos for catching "lunker" bass.

Another fishing writer of the early twentieth century is philosopher A. A. Luce, a native of Gloucestershire who spent most of his adult life in Ireland, a professor at Trinity College. While Luce can be described as closer to the balance struck by Walton than is Dunne, he is far more concerned with overcoming the fish and far less concerned with real introspection than one finds the Americans of the same period and beyond. This fact is well illustrated by comparing a passage from the foreword by American Datus Proper to the 1993 reprint of Luce's *Fishing and Thinking*:

The fishing comes before the thinking, he [Luce] insisted. You may go out simply to fish with one hand and pick wild raspberries with the other, but you find yourself becoming part of the four-dimensional world of sense and spirit. You get to know the river by entering it, in the manner of Plato. You cast over wine-dark waters, and your fly falls as falls the fancy on a perfect phrase. In time you achieve the philosophers' dream—action at a distance. By then you are fishing a long line and thinking long, long thoughts. (vii)

In contrast to Proper's rather ethereal, mystical view of fishing-thinking, Luce is, as a good follower of George Berkeley, considerably more didactic and reductive, a tendency that is especially notable in his final chapter on "The Ethics of Angling," yet is nevertheless present from the first chapter. Luce, like Dunne, eschews the traditional celebratory opening and begins his account with "My Best Day on the River," in which he, with no vanity apparent, describes a day when, inexplicably, the trout rose to everything he laid on the water. In attempting to explain why he might have such an exceptional experience on the day described in chapter one, Luce avoids the slightest hint of mysticism. There are none of the "long, long thoughts" that Proper describes, but rather a return to solid empirical foundations:

> The question looks well beyond one particular day and its personal interest; and the answer touches on the why and the wherefore of angling experiences that all anglers meet on their best days and their worst. For one cannot hope to understand and explain the particular experience of a special day without a good deal of general knowledge about the way of a trout with a fly. (18)

In short, Luce suggests, there is no ineffable experience on the water. There is simply an experience for which one's stock of knowledge is inadequate. Later, he again sounds an empiricist tone: "In fishing you just never know. The angler must 'fish and find out'" (9).

Lest Luce be cast in too stodgy a manner, his attitude toward Yeats illumines another, somewhat less didactic aspect of his personality. In the section of his book describing Yeats's country, he spends considerable time dealing with the poem "The Fisherman." In the poem, Yeats encounters a

> freckled man who goes
> To a grey place on a hill
> In grey Connemara clothes
> At dawn to cast his flies.

The poet, after his encounter with the fisherman, presents his writing to the general public:

> The craven man in his seat,
> The insolent unreproved,
> And no knave brought to book
> Who has won a drunken cheer.

Finding this audience unworthy, the poet remembers the fisherman and vows,

Before I am old
I shall have written him one
Poem maybe as cold
And passionate as the dawn. (61–62)

Luce praises this poem, calling it a difficult one to fathom; it is neither mystical nor weird; but it is strange, sui generis, and baffling. The mists of morning twilight hang around it; the language is simple, but the meaning is complex and obscure. The poem is by an angler, about an angler, and it has some deep meaning for anglers, if we could find out what that meaning is (80).

What Luce determines that meaning to be, though, is less than one might have expected from the foregoing. Yeats suggests, according to Luce, that if all the poet-narrator's readers were like the angler of the title, they would listen. He determines that perhaps Yeats chose angling because the angler experiences objectivity and a sense of control over an object (82). Luce seems to dismiss the "mists of morning twilight" and any hint of mysticism rather summarily, ascribing objectivity as a desired goal of one of the English language's most mystical and least objectively inclined poets.

Clearly, for Yeats, angling is not simply a matter of catching one's dinner. On the contrary, the sport provides a possibility to go beyond the obvious and to make a connection with profundities that have remained hidden. This view by Yeats can be seen to contradict one of Byron's criticisms of angling, that of single-mindedness toward the catch, yet Yeats's verse cannot completely refute Byron's attacks. The criticism, while perhaps overstated, is certainly based on a kernel of truth. Byron's other criticism, cruelty, is also taken up by both Dunne and Luce.

For Dunne, the issue of cruelty seems to hearken back to ideas of chivalry. "Unless your quarry be afforded a reasonable chance of escape, you are apt to feel yourself uncomfortably akin to a butcher," he says (1924,103). This sentiment, that the challenge of fly fishing is what makes it worthwhile, is prevalent in many writers on both sides of the Atlantic, but it lends itself to an argument by extension. If one feels more like a butcher as the odds shift away from the fish, then the contents of these books, dedicated to helping one improve angling skills, would seem self-defeating.

A. A. Luce, as one might expect, is less prone to logical fallacy. In "The Ethics of Angling" he takes on the charge of cruelty with considerable vigor: "People with a conscience who love their fishing rod are placed in a sad dilemma, as long as the question [regarding the cruelty of fishing] remains unanswered" (173). He begins with a definition: "Cruelty is the voluntary infliction of unnecessary or avoidable pain" (174). His argument seems straightforward enough until it reaches a turn that will shock virtually any serious, contemporary angler:

> It may look paradoxical at first sight to hold that it is cruel to hook and release trout, and not cruel to hook and kill them; but such is the case. Cruelty is largely in the mind and motive, and it is just here that the primary object of angling becomes of importance for both theory and practice. The primary object of justifiable angling is to catch fish for food; there are various pleasures incidental to angling; but they cannot justify the infliction of pain or death. (180)

Luce does not take up the issue of the unnecessary nature of the pain and suffering that an angler inflicts on the fish. In his view, if the fish is bound for the angler's plate, then fishing cannot be cruel. One wonders if this accomplished logician would have reached the same conclusion had he fished the heavily fished waters of New York's Beaverkill River in 1990, rather than relatively empty waters in rural Ireland. He argues, typical of the British school, with the reductive logic of Descartes, where North American writers would be more apt to use thought patterns drawn from Lao Tzu.

William Humphrey, an American, upon traveling to and fishing in England, noted certain facets of the country's fishing that shed considerable light on the attitudes described above:

> Nowhere is the class division more sharply drawn than in the national pastime. "Fishing in Britain," says the pamphlet sent me by The British Travel and Holiday Association, "falls in three classes: game, sea, and

coarse." Read: upper, middle, and lower. Trout taken from the public water here must be returned; they are the property of Mr. Mitchell that have strayed. Only coarse fish may be kept by the coarse. (1990, 253)

A survey of the three classes of angling in Britain, carried out in the early 1980s, asked a number of anglers from each class which among a group of reasons for pursuing their sport were the most important. All three groups included such items as "peace of mind" and "adventure and excitement"; only the coarse anglers omitted the item "take home food" from their top ten, while only they included the item "learn about new things" (Haworth 1983, 188–89). One would, of course, expect quite the opposite results. Stereotypes suggest that the working-class angler by the Mersey or the canal is fishing for huge carp that will feed the entire family, yet Howell Raines describes these anglers as "the most militant catch-and-release fishermen in the world. The distance they have advanced beyond the Tweedy Gents in environmental consciousness would have to be measured in light-years" (100).

Fishing in Britain is inextricably tied to the land and more precisely to the ownership of land. The fish in the stream that Humphrey fished are not viewed, as they might be in the United States and Canada, as a public trust over which one has an obligation of good stewardship, but as the "personal property, every one of them, of Mr. 'Porky' Mitchell, the meat-pie king. Eighty-five hundred pounds sterling he paid for the fishing in three miles of the stream for ten years" (Humphrey 1990, 252).

Humphrey also notes a curious aspect of British language in regards to the verbiage of fishing: "One does not catch a salmon. One kills a salmon. The distinction resembles that preserved in English between the verbs 'to murder' and 'to assassinate': ordinary citizens are murdered, leaders are assassinated. So with the King of Fish. He is not caught, like your perch or your pike or your lowly pickerel. He is killed" (258). One does not find just the salmon being "killed" in Britain, however. In many British texts, the verb *to kill* is used where an American would, even if intending to consume the fish, use the word *catch*.

It is generally agreed that while fly fishing enjoyed its birth and adolescence in Britain, its best practitioners are now and have been for some years those working the waters of North America, and just as the best of angling expertise has made its way to the Catskills or the Yellowstone, so the deepest and most rewarding angling writing has made the passage as well. Bryn Hammond, in his excellent treatise on the contemporary trout-fishing culture, notes a missing ingredient in recent British works:

> British angling writing has often been redolent with the nostalgia of past fishing events. Rarely, however, during the past fifty or so years have many British fishing writers explored the introspective *why?*, as in why men fish. It is almost as if they take it for granted their readers know and understand full well, without being told. I suspect it is more to do with two prime, though dissimilar reasons. To begin with, the genre has tended to produce thoroughly practical anglers, averse to too much wonderment about it. Secondly, it is uncommonly difficult to do. (1994, 11)

American writers, as will be seen in the following pages, have not ignored the question of why one fishes, nor have they, as a whole, become blind to the wonderment of their sport. Certainly in the years between the appearance of Berners's *Treatise* and the beginning of the twentieth century one would look to Britain for the continuation of the tradition of the literature of angling, but in recent years this has shifted. England is the land of Walton, but the United States is home to virtually every significant writer following in Walton's tradition. Hammond notes this move and the place that it has reserved for the land of Walton:

> Until recently it was generally Americans who made the pilgrimage across the Atlantic to fish in Britain, partly to escape the frenzied car-chasing of hatchery trucks on some of the more popular streams, partly as real pilgrims to fish in such fabled waters as the Test or Itchen or Dove—or even in stillwaters such as Blagdon. American flyfishermen, by and large, are generally more piscatorially literate and well-read than their British counterparts, and seek out and absorb the timeless redolence of well-remembered fishing books along with their fishing. It is part of fishing as far as they are concerned, and an important part at that—perhaps also they regard this pilgrimage to the historical cradle of fly fishing as being good for their souls. (118)

Something of an exception to Hammond's generalization can be found in Neil Patterson, whose *Chalkstream Chronicle* details a year in the midst of "The Hollow," a web of English chalkstreams. Patterson evokes memories of recent American fishing writers, yet he still presents many distinctively British attitudes. He lives on the river. He speaks of those who own the fishing rights to the area (1995, 89). Despite these reservations, which derive chiefly from the geography of his country, Patterson shows that influences on fishing writing can flow in both directions across the Atlantic.

R. B. Marston, in his 1894 bibliographical and historical study of Walton and his forebears, laments the flow of the early editions of Walton's work to United States collectors, noting that they will probably never come back to England (1894, 8). At about the same moment in history, Marston could have witnessed the crest in fly fishing expertise passing from the waters of the Test and the Tweed to the wilder climes of the Beaverkill and points farther west. Perhaps Marston understood what was happening as he wrote, observing that "Walton is not out of place at Chicago. Extremes meet; and we have, as it were, a precedent for it in the contrast between Walton's calm life and the turbulent, terrible times in which he lived" (105).

Both Berners's and Walton's works were produced in times of great upheaval in England, the former at the close of the Wars of the Roses and the latter during the English Civil War. While the past century has been far from placid for the British, perhaps it is noteworthy that Walton's mantle has passed to another country that has been still attempting to define itself and realize its potential.

Interlude 2

The Dangler

FROM *the year that we sold the lake house to the time of my initiation in the secrets of fly fishing, my fishing was frustrated, shore-bound, and usually performed in the company of Bill, a fishing buddy I will refer to as My Brother-in-law the Dangler. His appellation derived from a fishing expedition I did not witness, but which has gone down into the annals of legend within our family. Only a select few of us know the truth of the matter.*

Several years ago, Bill grudgingly accompanied his long-suffering wife on a trip some thirty miles up Interstate 35 to the farm of her Uncle Bob. Bill would probably have flatly rejected the trip but for two extenuating facts: He didn't want to seem like a lousy husband in the eyes of the uncle, and the uncle maintains a large pond stocked with enormous catfish. Needless to say, Bill just happened to throw his stoutest rod in the back of the truck before they hit the road that Saturday.

Catfish, if you were not aware, can grow to phenomenal sizes. In Osceola, Missouri, there's a bait shop with the state-record blue catfish mounted above the cash register. This brute is nearly six feet long and looks nearly as omnivorous as the overall-clad, Twinkie-snarfing man mountain who minds the counter.

The cats in Bill's uncle's pond are not quite that huge, but they are good-sized owing to the fact that the uncle feeds them on a daily basis. "I just hate the idea of the big ones eating up all the little ones," he explains when pressed on why he doesn't just let nature and the existing food supply regulate the population. Having seen both, Bill affirms that the big ones could easily gulp down half a dozen little ones in the midst of a yawn.

Feeding fish, of course, ensures a larger-than-normal population as well as larger-than-normal fish, but it also makes the overstuffed residents of the pond turn up their whiskered snouts at such traditional catfish fare as stinkbait and beef liver. On the day in question, Bill sat fuming on the bank for several hours as every fish in the pond inspected and quickly rejected his hook-laced offering. He scarcely managed to contain his frustration as Uncle Bob ambled to his side.

"Had much luck?" Bob asked, sending a stream of Red Man and saliva arcing into the weeds.

"Not much," Bill answered.

Bob glanced around the area, apparently searching for something. "How many you got?"

Bill shifted the pole from right to left hand. "Well . . . uh, not exactly, uh, none."

"No keepers, eh?" Bob carried on, shifting the tobacco in his cheek.

"Yeah, basically," Bill replied, his eyes fixed on the bobber that floated ten feet from the shore.

Uncle Bob apparently understood Bill's predicament because he instructed Bill to reel in his line and watch as the fish enjoyed their supper. "They eat like crazy when I'm feeding 'em," he explained.

As the pellets of feed struck the water, the surface of the pond erupted in an angry fit. Flashes of fish appeared for a moment as the feed disappeared. After a couple of moments, Bill's eyes focused on the center of the melee. There, amid the chaos of churning water, he could make out several cavernous mouths, open and gaping for the feed to fall into.

After church the next day, when we all gathered at Bill's house to eat catfish, he asked the blessing on "this food that You allowed me to catch." The whole family ate all we cared to eat and we had barely consumed half of the monster that Bill pulled out of Uncle Bob's pond. I have to say that on that Sunday, eating that fish, I was impressed and maybe just a little bit jealous. It was only a week or two later that Bill confided to me that he had caught the fish during that feeding frenzy by dropping an unbaited hook into the biggest, most gaping mouth he could find and setting the hook quickly.

Some people catch fish by casting, some by trolling. Bill caught his monster by dangling, hence his nickname, my brother-in-law the dangler. I must say now, however, that if I sound a trifle superior in calling him that, I am being unfair, for I, too, have spent plenty of time as a dangler.

Dangling, you see, is not just to be performed on the side of a farm pond full of catfish that desperately need to diet. Dangling is, instead, a frame of mind that insists that fishing is all about and only about catching fish. For years, the spotty fishing I performed was all about dominance, about proving myself as an outdoorsman and master of nature. When I caught a seventeen-and-a-half-inch striper below the spillway of a nearby lake, it didn't bother me that the fish was illegal by half an inch. I knew that I could bluff my way out of the situation should the Conservation Department make an appearance, but perhaps more to the point, I knew that such a fish, although not all that impressive by striper standards, would be sufficient to amaze and delight my wife and, most important, my kids.

This fish had the misfortune of latching onto a chartreuse grub I had been dragging along the bottom for a couple of hours at the end of a number of consecutive Saturdays when I had caught exactly nothing. Every Saturday, Bill and I would roll into my driveway at about eleven to find both of our wives and all of our kids waiting for us. The kids, each and every Saturday, would burst out of the house the second we hit the driveway. And each and every Saturday, each and every kid felt compelled to ask the question that both Bill and I dreaded to hear: "How many did you catch?" It wasn't, "Did you catch any?" with its implicit acceptance of a negative answer. No, it was, "How many did you catch?" with its clear rejection of zero as an acceptable reply. Each and every Saturday, I felt the pangs of shame as my failure as father, fisher, and male was trumpeted in front of my children. Is it any wonder that I should become a dangler? Can't one call this justifiable?

3

Upstream: The American Fork

WHILE Old World roots, most notably biblical and English sources, inform American writing in general and fishing writing specifically, there are certain indigenous sources that have similarly affected the fishing tradition in the New World. One of these, the Native American tradition, existed independently of any European contact. The other important source, Transcendentalism, exists as an American version of Romanticism.

The Native American

If the thesis regarding fishing representing the border territory between humans and animals is valid, then one would expect a significant amount of support for it from the literature and oral tradition of more primitive peoples. Since the indigenous inhabitants of North America were being exposed to Europeans for the first time only at about the time that Walton was publishing his editions, one would hope to find this support in a plentiful and relatively unpolluted form. Such is simply not the case. For all the historical significance drawn from the impact of the Iroquois governmental system on the Constitution of the United States, it is apparent that Native Americans were neither in a position nor clearly desirous to infuse their tradition into what would become mainstream American culture.

One might describe the effect of Native American culture on mainstream American culture (and on the culture of fly fishing) by returning to the previous metaphor of the confluent streams. While biblical and English might be described as clearly identifiable tributaries flowing together to create a larger stream, the entry of Native American influences would have to be compared with seepage and ground water. That the Native American influence is found in the eventual river is undeniable, but to identify precisely its entry into the tradition, as we can, for example, point to 1653 as Walton's entry, is not practical.

The Native American material that makes its way into the literature in question often comes indirectly. It is filtered, in the way that *Black Elk Speaks* is an original account filtered by a European editor. Due to this misdirection, delay, and filtration, the product is often not nearly as pure as one would hope. The concern of this study, however, is not with the way things should be, but with the way that they are. Clearly, there are numerous identifiable Native American influences in Transcendentalism, in nature writing, and ultimately in the fly-fishing stream.

One significant area in which Native American attitudes seem to surface in fishing writing is in the attitude toward the prey. Where the European tradition typically sees the fish as an adversary to be overcome by guile, skill, or strength, the Native American tradition emphasizes arriving at a connection or sympathy with the fish. Among the magical beliefs of the Cherokee is found a sacred formula for catching large fish. Among the things to be said while chewing a bit of Venus Flytrap and baiting the hook with it is, "Our spittle shall be in agreement," meaning that there will be such a close sympathy between fish and fisher that their spittle will be as one person's (Mooney 1992, 374–75). In this same vein one finds the notion that "once upon a time man and animals talked with one another on this continent" (Martin 1978, 156).

The animism of many Native American tribes infused power in the significant objects of life. Where for Christian Europe, the fish was a symbol, for the Native American the fish was simultaneously symbol and that symbolized. Certain tribes performed bone rites in which hunters and fishers arranged the bones of game or fish subsequent to the meal in order to assure the rebirth of the animal. These included seasonal rites, such as the salmon rites on the Northwest Coast, and occasional rites that might be performed before the hunt or after each kill (Hultkrantz 1979, 104–5).

James Frazer describes the manner by which the indigenous people of British Columbia produced fish in times of need: "If the fish do not come in due season, and the Indians are hungry, a Nootka wizard will make an image of a swimming fish and put it into the water in the direction from which the fish generally appear. This ceremony, accompanied by a prayer to the fish to come, will cause them to arrive at once" (45). He also describes the manner in which the Kwakiutl Indians believe that salmon, upon their death, return to the salmon country to be reborn. In respect for this belief, the Kwakiutl are careful to return the uneaten remains of their catch to the sea to aid in this reanimation and ensure a future catch. The Ottawa, believing that the soul of the dead fish would transmigrate to others, never burned the bones of their catch for fear of offending the soul's new inhabitant, while the Huron believed that burning the bones would release the soul to warn other fish of their fiery fate if caught (Frazer 1959, 553). In short, Frazer emphasizes the respect that the American Indian held for the prey. Wise husbandry would be expected from a people dependent on the continuation of a species, but some of these practices go beyond wise husbandry into honor and respect.

Calvin Martin points to the onset of European contact and the initiation of trade as the time of change. According to Martin, "the conjuror and the drum became obsolete when Nature became inarticulate—despiritualized." At this time, according to Martin, a fundamental shift occurred in the attitude of these peoples toward nature: "Wildlife were hounded without quarter not just because their hides were valuable for trading purposes but because they were now considered man's implacable enemy; they were deaf and dumb and treacherous" (1978, 156).

While Martin's observations might be correct, there was a two-way, albeit unbalanced, traffic going on at this time. Although Native Americans were adopting, at least somewhat, the economic attitudes of the Europeans, the Europeans were slowly accepting certain Native American philosophical attitudes into the mainstream. Vine Deloria contrasts the location-based religions of Native Americans with a time-based Christianity. Both these orientations find expression in the fishing, nature, and environmental writings of recent years. The Indian-ecology ideal is seen in Faulkner's "The Bear," Cooper's *Leatherstocking Tales*, Francis Parkman's *France and England in North America* and *The Oregon Trail*, Melville's *Moby Dick*, Cather's *Death Comes for the Archbishop*, and the Nick Adams stories of Hemingway. "Clearly the *bon sauvage*–attuned to Nature idea has long been a favorite device in American literature" (Martin 1978, 161).

Ultimately, the Native American legacy, with varying degrees of accuracy, has receded into a national consciousness that is not altogether certain what to make of the bequest. Barry Lopez touches on this ambivalence in his writings on the Anasazi:

> For many in the Southwest today the Anasazi are a vague and nebulous passage in the history of human life. For others . . . they are an intense reflection of the land, a puzzle to be addressed the way a man might try to understand the now-departed curlew. For still others they are a spiritual repository, a mysterious source of strength born of their intimacy with the Colorado Plateau. (1989, 175)

The Transcendental

To examine the impact of Transcendentalism on nature writing and later the literature of fishing, one is drawn most closely into the orbit of Henry David Thoreau. Thoreau takes the ideas presented by Emerson in *Nature*, develops and applies them. Emerson, although a religious seeker, found Unitarianism unsatisfying since Unitarianism had not only lost its vigorous emotional piety in its movement away from Calvinism, but had found itself defending the sovereignty of reason and free will at the same time that it strengthened itself on the determinism of Lockean psychology and the mechanism of Newtonian physics. Ultimately, while claiming to be a rational faith, with nothing but natural law for its guide, it had irrationally insisted on the historicity of miracles. By Emerson's time, Unitarianism could be described as a faith at second hand, building on the testimony of other men. This decay left Emerson seeking for an original relation to the universe, a project that was identical with seeking a direct communion with God; the transcendentalists' hunger for Reality was a hunger for God. This desire for direct communion resurfaces a century later in fly-fishing literature, as writer-anglers attempt to forge a direct knowledge of themselves, transcendent truth, and nature.

Where the British were viewing nature as an adversary, Emerson had made nature a moral teacher and the most effective means by which man could be educated; he had suggested that the end of man's relationship with nature was an improvement of character, that character and being joined into one. Emerson stopped little short of suggesting the divinity of man. One critic describes the impact of this school of thought as follows:

> The Transcendentalism that shaped and sustained Thoreau's youthful aspirations was a revolt of such depth and magnitude that its force is still alive today. Rejecting most of the philosophical assumptions of the eighteenth century, it attempted to reorient the possibilities of life, to give the individual new powers and a new stage for action; and its urgency was felt especially in America where its desire to make all things new promised so much for the new democracy. (Paul 1972, 3)

Sherman Paul, in the introductory chapter to his study of Thoreau, attempts to outline the importance of Emerson's work on Thoreau:

> The major shift that *Nature* described was from outer to inner dominion, from sensation to experience—a process of taking up the Not-me by the Me. Mind, ideas, consciousness were primary, and the external world existed to be assimilated as the stuff of thought. The cognitive act was not a knowing of things, but a having, an inner possession of them. As much of the external world as man transformed into himself and radiated with meaning, so much did he truly possess: and again, this was not knowledge, but an acquisition of being, an enlargement of self. (7)

While the connection between the British tradition of fishing writing and Thoreau might seem tenuous, Emerson made it overt in a "Preliminary Note" to Thoreau's essay "Natural History of Massachusetts," where Emerson describes his protégé as

> a near neighbor and friend of ours, dear also to the Muses, a native and an inhabitant of the town of Concord, who readily undertook to give us such comments as he had made on these books, and, better still, notes of his own conversation with nature in the woods and waters of this town. With all thankfulness we begged our friend to lay down the oar and fishing line, which none can handle better, and assume the pen, that Isaak Walton and White of Selborne might not want a successor. (19)

Two of Thoreau's works are especially significant to the present study. One is, of course, *Walden*, but before taking up that landmark of Americanism, it is worthwhile to examine an earlier and less widely studied work, *A Week on the Concord and Merrimack Rivers*. In that first attempt at a book-length manuscript, Thoreau endeavors to use the passing of a journey as the organizing principle and raison d'être for a series of observations about nature, humankind, and their interrelations. Although the observations seem to flow randomly from the accidental events of the journey, they achieve by the return to Concord a sense of unity and wholeness, allowing this work a claim to greater integration than its more famous successor, *Walden*. This very form, in which the author observes something in nature, apparently with no preparation, and then draws some larger philosophical point from the encounter is a device used by many modern fly-fishing writers. The essays written by Nick Lyons at the end of each issue of *Fly Fisherman* magazine are normally examples of this genre. One such essay, "On a Small Creek," will serve to illustrate the point. In this case, Lyons tells of returning to a creek he had fished many years earlier. After watching a "skinny, lanky kid" catch a twenty-inch brown trout in a spot where he had lost one of the same size years before, Lyons feels compelled to talk to the boy:

> I say I've just been looking, that I haven't fished and won't this after-noon. It all sounds hollow—or worse.
> The boy looks at my graphite rod and Hardy reel, at me—sharply in the eye—smiles, and begins to turn.
> He says, over his shoulder, "Yeah, I see." Before I can pontificate about killing trout or bemoan the loss of my own innocence, and while I try to stop shaking, he goes dancing down the little creek that had simply been a good place to spend a summer afternoon and catch breakfast. (95)

One might, of course, note that Thoreau is not alone in drawing pro-found conclusions from mundane encounters in the early years of the nineteenth century. Such a move is exactly what Wordsworth seems to suggest in the "Preface to the *Lyrical Ballads*," yet there is a different mood involved as Thoreau pursues "emotion recollected in tranquillity." The of-ferings of Americans from Thoreau to Lyons, at least when working at their best, seem less contrived and more genuine than those of their British counterparts.

As Thoreau and his brother made their way down the Concord River to its confluence with the Merrimack, they marked a number of sights that signified the presence of humans in this place before, but throughout the essay, an air of wildness seems to hang over the natural world. Human-crafted things are described as disappearing in the enormousness of nature, either quickly, like the Carlisle Bridge, disappearing into the distance, the surface of which "was reduced to a line's breadth, and appeared like a cob-web gleaming in the sun" (150), or gradually, as with the impediments to the spawning movements of fish that humans have built across the river:

"Perchance, after a few thousands of years, if the fishes will be patient, and pass their summers elsewhere meanwhile, nature will have leveled the Billerica dam, and the Lowell factories, and the Grass-ground River run clear again, to be explored by new migratory shoals" (156).

Fishing plays a part, as one might expect, in the life of the two rivers that the two Thoreaus travel. At one point, Thoreau describes a sight that is turned into a totemistic image: "Here and there might be seen a pole sticking up, to mark the place where some fisherman had enjoyed unusual luck, and in return had consecrated his rod to the deities who preside over these shallows" (150). While these poles had belonged to Europeans, the consecration of them to the river gods seems something much more appropriate to the Native Americans inhabiting the area.

Early in their journey, Thoreau describes two fishermen, one that they see and one who is remembered. In describing the first angler, he notes the value of fishing for drawing people into the recesses of nature:

> Late in the afternoon we passed a man on the shore fishing with a long birch pole, its silvery bark left on, and a dog at his side, rowing so near as to agitate his cork with our oars, and drive away luck for a season; and when we had rowed a mile as straight as an arrow, with our faces turned towards him, and the bubbles in our wake still visible on the tranquil surface, there stood the fisher still with his dog, like statues under the other side of the heavens. . . . Thus, by one bait or another, Nature allures inhabitants into all her recesses. (150–51)

The second fisherman, whose memory is apparently evoked by the passing of the first, is described at length, passing during that description from simply an old man, through an object of pity or melancholy, to a sort of mystic status, to whom Thoreau refers as "the Walton of this stream" (152).

> A straight old man he was, who took his way in silence through the meadows, having passed the period of communication with his fellows; his old experienced coat hanging long and straight and brown as the yellow pine bark, glittering with so much smothered sunlight, if you stood near enough, no work of art but naturalized at length. I often discovered him unexpectedly amid the pads and the gray willows when he moved, fishing in some old country method—for youth and age then went a-fishing to-

gether—full of incommunicable thoughts, perchance about his own Tyne and Northumberland. He was always to be seen in serene afternoon haunting the river, and almost rustling with the sedge; so many sunny hours in an old man's life, entrapping silly fish; almost grown to be the sun's familiar; what need had he of hat or raiment any, having served out his time, and seen through such thin disguises? I have seen how his coeval fates rewarded him with the yellow perch and yet I thought his luck was not in proportion to his years; and I have seen when, with slow steps and weighed down with aged thoughts, he disappeared with his fish under his low-roofed house on the skirts of the village. I think nobody else saw him; nobody else remembers him now, for he soon after died, and migrated to new Tyne streams. His fishing was not a sport, nor solely a means of subsistence, but a sort of solemn sacrament and withdrawal from the world, just as the aged read their Bibles. (152)

Although Dame Juliana Berners was (supposedly) a nun and Izaak Walton was a devout Anglican, neither of these two, or any other British writer yet encountered, describes fishing in terms that are of such a spiritual nature. Perhaps Thoreau can call fishing a "sort of solemn sacrament" because of his own rejection of more conventional sacraments, but he prefigures a wide use of fishing as a very active metaphor for religion and spiritual life in American writers, probably most notable in the opening of Norman Maclean's *A River Runs through It*, when Maclean remarks that "there was no clear line between religion and fly fishing."

Thoreau, though, might have drawn a third aspect into this analogy, the life of contemplation. Sherman Paul points to the passage concerning the old fisherman to make exactly this point:

Considering also the life of the fisherman, it was possible for Thoreau to describe his own vocation, the life of contemplation. Fishing, he said, was "a sort of solemn sacrament and withdrawal from the world"—as Izaak Walton had said, a contemplative man's recreation. And science, Thoreau went on to say, thinking of science in terms of the Indian wisdom of the "Natural History" and of his own study of the fishes, was "only a more contemplative man's recreation." Thinking of vocations in light of the transcendental notion of the ages of man from out-of-door life to consciousness, he claimed that every age had its characteristic vocation, that in the spring of history, man was a fisher and a hunter. (1972, 214)

Paul goes on to suggest that the lone fisherman on the bank was used by Thoreau not only to outline his sense that he lived in a degenerate era but also to suggest what attitude the reader might take toward his expedition: "Because fishing belonged to the natural era, it also provided Thoreau with a historical reference by holding up against the heroism of Concord in the past the ignoble lives of the present; and the lone fisherman whom he passed as he left Concord not only suggested what followed of fish and fishermen, but stood as a symbol of the quiet heroism of his own under-taking" (214).

It is not to overstate the case to suggest that the distinctiveness of all American fishing writing flows from these few paragraphs. By calling the old fisherman "the Walton of this stream" Thoreau not only elevates the old man, but also transforms Walton, who, while on English shores had been simply a wise and thoughtful fisherman, but who, in the hands of Thoreau, became something more like a prophet or mystic. Clearly, Thoreau does not develop this idea to its fullest and it is unclear whether he had any real sense of the import that others would draw from these paragraphs, yet here one can find the germ for a development that would take place over a century and a half in the United States.

Another aspect of *A Week on the Concord and Merrimack Rivers* that has attained great significance for the literature of fishing is the attitude to-ward nature that Thoreau presents. "Art is not tame, and Nature is not wild, in the ordinary sense. A perfect work of man's art would also be wild or natural in a good sense. Man tames nature only that he may at last make her more free even than he found her, though he may never yet have succeeded" (194). This attitude, while clearly deriving from Emer-son's thought, also seems to tap the influence (or at least perceived influence) of Native American ideas. This is evident in Thoreau's de-scription of one point in the journey, at which the brothers reached a par-ticularly isolated point on the river: "On either side, the primeval forest stretches away uninterrupted to Canada, or to the 'South Sea'; to the white man a drear and howling wilderness, but to the Indian a home, adapted to his nature, and cheerful as the smile of the Great Spirit" (200).

The pages of *A Week* also suggest one further hallmark of later American fishing literature, the focus on paradox and division. The end of the "Monday" section of the book consists entirely of an extended series of contrasts. Over the course of several pages, Thoreau engages in a qualitative comparison of various levels of life, working from the individual to the level of entire cultures. He begins by examining the qualities of various vocations, focusing especially on the level of action and contemplation involved in each. He contrasts leisure with busy-ness. From this level, Thoreau moves to an evaluation of different ages. The Indian and the colonial past are seen as a golden age to be preferred over the present age of industry and its possible future. Finally, his comparison reaches its greatest scope as he discusses universal history, comparing East and West, Orient and Occident.

Looking more closely at one example of this catalog of contrasts one finds Thoreau's attitude toward activity and reflection. For the British, these are conflicting values. Both are worthy, but they do not coexist. Walton, the bait fisherman, is able to relax, but for his fly-fishing successors, the prevailing value is vigor and activity. Thoreau, on the other hand, suggests that activity is useful only if it is underlaid with reflection. "Behind every man's busy-ness there should be a level of undisturbed serenity and industry, as within the reef encircling a coral isle there is always an expanse of still water" (219).

Rather than considering activity as an "other," Thoreau sought an integration of the disparate aspects of life: "One's vocation, therefore, placed him in time: to fish, or to excursion on the river, was a recreation appropriate to the Golden Age, a vocation that Thoreau subtly transformed, however, by blending the out-of-door life with the life of the mind" (Paul 1972, 214). Thoreau, therefore, attempts to blend the inwardness of the mind with the outwardness of nature, a move the British rarely approached.

Another case in which Thoreau seems to take a contradictory stand is when he suggests that the orator "is then most eloquent when most silent. He listens while he speaks, and is a hearer along with his audience" (226).

While this statement has nothing to do with fishing, there is a related tendency in fishing writing, which holds that silence speaks loudest.

Robert Stowell finds a further example of self-contradiction in Thoreau's attitudes toward maps: "Attraction and revulsion seem also to characterize his attitude toward maps. He must have been fascinated by them, for he never missed an opportunity to study a map and comment upon its accuracy" (1970, ix). The map is, of course, valuable only insofar as it reflects reality, an attribute that Thoreau sought in virtually every aspect of life. Stowell suggests that "most of his [Thoreau's] writings represent 'the pleasure of poetry' that geography afforded, so the maps in this Gazetteer are presumably some of the 'bald natural facts' that served as his raw material. The two elements, poetry and fact, mingled constantly in Thoreau's work and affected his personal behavior" (ix), yet it should not be ignored that the map is not the "bald natural fact," but simply a representation of that fact, just as the words that an author puts down on paper are merely representations of the author's meaning. Such a vicarious experience should be avoided, but is sometimes the only experience available. "A map . . . was of value to Thoreau as an artifact of experience; as he learned during his trip to Canada, it clarified 'what would otherwise have been left in a limbo of unintelligibility'" (Stowell 1970, ix–x).

As important as *A Week* is in terms of the direction it seems to have determined for American literature of fishing, one cannot consider Thoreau fully while ignoring *Walden*. One writer explains Thoreau's move from river to pond:

> Although Thoreau briefly considered making his Walden experiment
> along the trout brook at Baker Farm, he was a stillwater thinker at heart,
> and so settled for a time by the water that best reflected his intellect and
> imagination. I find him better company on wild water, and would rather
> paddle with him on the West Branch of the Penobscot, where he met the
> natural world on its own terms, than sit with him at Walden Pond, where
> he made of nature a studied still life, albeit a beautiful and thoughtful one.
> (Camuto 1990, 232)

Where *A Week* was an experiment in travel writing fused with social commentary, *Walden* is a much larger part of Thoreau's overall project, repre-

senting his determination to identify and meet the basic facts of life, to reduce life to its lowest terms, and to find its essence.

If one looks to *Walden* for fishing stories, there is not much to find, but
that which is present is significant. The one passage that is most essential
comes in the section on "The Ponds":

> These experiences were very memorable and valuable to me, anchored in
> forty feet of water, and twenty or thirty rods from the shore, surrounded
> sometimes by thousands of small perch and shiners, dimpling the surface
> with their tails in the moonlight, and communicating by a long flaxen line
> with mysterious nocturnal fishes which had their dwelling forty feet below,
> or sometimes dragging sixty feet of line about the pond as I drifted in the
> gentle night breeze, now and then feeling a slight vibration along it, in-
> dicative of some life prowling about its extremity, of dull uncertain blun-
> dering purpose there, and slow to make up its mind. At length you slowly
> raise, pulling hand over hand, some horned pout squeaking and squirming
> to the upper air. It was very queer, especially in dark nights, when your
> thoughts had wandered to vast and cosmogonal themes in other spheres,
> to feel this faint jerk, which came to interrupt your dreams and link you to
> Nature again. It seemed as if I might next cast my line upward into the air,
> as well as downward into this element, which was scarcely more dense.
> Thus I caught two fishes as it were with one hook. (424)

Sherman Paul suggests that one compare this fishing section in *Walden*,
with its pithy "Thus I caught two fishes as it were with one hook," with
Melville's "The Mast-Head" and with the fishing in Hemingway's "Big
Two-Hearted River": "And although Thoreau never suggested that his
later fishing for the pond might be 'tragic,' what had made that fishing
necessary was" (1972, 337).

For Thoreau, there was nothing magical about fishing. What was magical and what has been co-opted by later fishing writers is the idea of the
primacy of direct experience. Probably the most famous passage from
Walden is the following:

> I went to the woods because I wished to live deliberately, to front only the
> essential facts of life, and see if I could not learn what it had to teach, and
> not, when I came to die, discover that I had not lived. I did not wish to
> live what was not life, living is so dear; nor did I wish to practice resigna-

tion, unless it was quite necessary. I wanted to live deep and suck out all the marrow of life, to live so sturdily and Spartan-like as to put to rout all that was not life. (343–44)

This bold bundle of aphorisms can be boiled down to the idea of direct experience. The land itself, according to Thoreau, is to be preferred to the map representing it. True knowledge can be had only by true and direct experience. This theme is echoed several times in the book. At one point, in talking of literature, Thoreau suggests that "[t]he works of the great poets have never yet been read by mankind, for only great poets can read them. They have only been read as the multitude read the stars, at most astrologically, not astronomically" (356). In order to know fully a thing, then, one must not simply come to it and experience it tangentially, but must be fully a part of it, an idea suggesting the attitudes toward bullfighting in *The Sun Also Rises,* where only the aficionado can truly enjoy and understand the sport. Coming back to this idea a few chapters later, Thoreau applies it to a completely different field: "The fruits do not yield their true flavor to the purchaser of them, nor to him who raises them for the market. There is but one way to obtain it, yet few take that way. If you would know the flavor of huckleberries, ask the cowboy or the partridge. It is a vulgar error to suppose that you have tasted huckleberries who never plucked them" (422).

For Thoreau, one can clearly see, direct experience was the only true experience; thus the angler, whatever failings he might have in Thoreau's eyes, is to be admired for being at work in the gathering of direct experience. In one passage from *Walden,* two different anglers are described as possessing something of the ineffable quality that Thoreau so highly values:

Occasionally, after my hoeing was done for the day, I joined some impatient companion who had been fishing on the pond since morning, as silent and motionless as a duck or a floating leaf, and, after practicing various kinds of philosophy, had concluded commonly, by the time I arrived, that he belonged to the ancient sect of Cenobites. There was one older man, an excellent fisher and skilled in all kinds of woodcraft, who was pleased to look upon my house as a building erected for the convenience of fishermen; and I was equally pleased when he sat in my doorway to arrange his lines. Once in a while we sat together on the pond, he at one end of the boat, and I at the other; but not many words passed between us, for he had grown deaf in his later years, but he occasionally hummed a psalm, which harmonized well enough with my philosophy. Our intercourse was thus altogether one of unbroken harmony, far more pleasing to remember than if it had been carried on by speech. (422–23)

The first of these anglers is associated with an ancient religious order, an attachment that Thoreau, with his often nostalgic attitude toward things past, must be assumed to have meant positively. The other man is able to communicate in a manner that transcends words by simply humming a hymn. Taken together, all the representations of anglers that Thoreau has offered in the preceding passages might lead one to assume that the angler served as a sort of archetypal mystic to be closely emulated, yet counterbalancing the weights of Thoreau the romantic and the mystic are those of Thoreau the empiricist and the scientist. Decidedly unromantic is the following inventory of species that is offered for the pond:

There have been caught in Walden pickerel, one weighing seven pounds—to say nothing of another which carried off a reel with great velocity, which the fisherman safely set down at eight pounds because he did not see him—perch and pouts, some of each weighing over two pounds, shiners, chivins or roach (Leuciscus pulchellus), a very few breams, and a couple of eels, one weighing four pounds—I am thus particular because the weight of a fish is commonly its only title to fame, and these are the only eels I have heard of here—also, I have a faint recollection of a little fish some five inches long, with silvery sides and a greenish back, somewhat dace-like in its character, which I mention here chiefly to link my facts to fable. Nevertheless, this pond is not very fertile in fish. (432–33)

There is in this passage no sense of the fish as a brother creature, as was seen in the Native American myths. Likewise, there is no suggestion of the fish as a vehicle for divine insight, as in the biblical accounts. Instead, the weight of a fish is its only claim to fame.

Thoreau's attitude toward the pond could be equally as prosaic as that which he took toward the fish within it. In the spirit of Galileo, he shows his empirical bent in answering the question of the pond's depth. The townspeople, for want of testing their hypothesis, believed Walden pond to be bottomless, yet Thoreau, using a stone and a line, judged its depth at one hundred and two feet. "I am thankful that this pond was made deep and pure for a symbol. While men believe in the infinite some ponds will be thought to be bottomless" (528).

Thoreau, then, as a prototypical Transcendentalist, can be described, like the modern fly-fishing writer, as a divided person. He is, without a doubt, possessed of a certain mystical mindset, yet at the same time he can adopt and champion a scientific attitude toward nature. These two apparently contradictory forces coexist and do not strike the reader as mutually destructive. Thoreau seems to find the meeting point for these forces and to forge them together. This meeting point suggests Eliot's "still point of the turning world. Neither flesh nor fleshless" in "Burnt Norton" (1971, 15). For Thoreau, that apparently unattainable point is one of knowledge: "If we knew all the laws of Nature, we should need only one fact, or the description of one actual phenomenon, to infer all the particular results at that point" (531).

Without all the laws of nature, however, Thoreau is left to measure and count that which can be quantified and to write boldly and somewhat impressionistically about that which remains unknowable. The angler occupies a position attempting to straddle the gap left between the known and the unknown, and Thoreau, although not the most avid angler, occupies an analogous position, as he describes in his poem "Nature."

> O nature I do not aspire
> To be the highest in thy quire,
> To be a meteor in the sky
> Or comet that may range on high,
> Only a zephyr that may blow
> Among the reeds by the river low.
> Give me thy most privy place
> Where to run my airy race.
> In some withdrawn unpublic mead
> Let me sigh upon a reed,
> Or in the woods with leafy din
> Whisper the still evening in,

For I had rather be thy child
And pupil in the forest wild
Than be the king of men elsewhere
And most sovereign slave of care
To have one moment of thy dawn
Than share the city's year forlorn.
Some still work give me to do
Only be it near to you. (242)

Interlude 3

False Casts

I CAME *to fly fishing to fish deliberately, to suck out the essential marrow of fishing and seek its inner essence, so that when I came to die I would not find that I had not lived—or perhaps had not fished. I came to fly fishing to escape the factious swirl of civilized life, to find those things that were most elemental and irreducible.*

No. That wasn't it.

In my family there was little distinction made between fly fishing and life. One fished because one lived and lived because one fished. We lived at the confluence of mighty rivers and enormous lakes. By teaching the rhythm of fishing, my father sought to teach the rhythms of life, simple and steady despite their outward complexities.

No. That wasn't it either.

I actually came to fly fishing quite by accident. In the midst of academic pursuits (of which the present text represents a culmination) I found it necessary to arrive at that most difficult of fly selections, the dissertation topic. Having a basic idea dealing with some notion of peaceful rhetoric vaguely fixed in my mind, I proposed it in several different forms to my advisor, who rejected those forms in his polite but unambiguous manner. In each case, I would describe my idea to him. He would think for a moment, nod a couple of times, and say, "Well, you could do that." The emphasis on the word could rendered his response so conditional that it was evident to anyone with active brain cells that this was not the prudent choice.

After offering several such proposals to my advisor, I was, admittedly, growing restless. Never mind that each proposal was simply a recycled, rehashed version of the one before or that my advisor was attempting to save me (and himself) endless hours of tedium on an impossible topic. I was frustrated. That was why as I lay in bed one night, I made the following pronouncement to my wife: "I'm going to pitch two new ideas to him tomorrow. If he doesn't like either of those, then I'm going to say I want to do the literature of hunting and fishing." Such sarcasm, I supposed, might aptly convey my mental state.

As might be expected, my meeting the next afternoon moved through those two serious proposals very quickly. After detailing the second, I waited as his brow furrowed. In a moment, he spoke, "I guess you could do that one."

The dual emphases made my course irreversible. I took a deep breath. "I could always do the literature of hunting and fishing," I blurted, prepared to cower behind my books should the meeting grow ugly.

His eyes lit up. "Hey," he said, a slight smile dawning on his face. "You know, that's not bad. That's not bad at all." With that, he burst into a dizzying stream of possible directions I could attempt, books I should consult, persons who might serve on the committee, and the like. It was all I could do to jot down the notes as we narrowed the topic to fishing and then to fly fishing. In a few minutes, however, he paused for a breath and admitted that beyond Hemingway and Norman Maclean, he knew virtually nothing of the genre. "It sounds great, but I'm afraid you're somewhat on your own," he admonished as I left.

I found myself sitting upon the shore, fishing, but I had no guide. I knew little to nothing about fly fishing—in reality, I knew little to nothing about any kind of fishing—and I wasn't at all sure of how I might proceed either in the fishing or in the study of the literature. My guides, well meaning as they were, stood powerless to offer much assistance. For the literature, the guides were knowledgeable in nature writing, but couldn't bring much light to the fishing works. In the realm of fishing, my mentors were limited to my brother-in-law the dangler and my father, who hadn't let the frog lure see the light of day in twenty years. I was on my own.

Wading into the stream, the chill of spring-fed river water stung my legs through my waders. I held the requisite tools in my hand. The rod thrust out nine feet from my hand. Loops of flyline trailed from the rod and draped onto the swiftly flowing water. In a breast pocket I had safely stashed a thin plastic box full of all manner of flies. I couldn't recall their names and much less their supposed uses. I even wore a cool hat.

The river—I probably would have called it a creek—stretched away to the right and left of me. Pools and riffles, eddies and calm places were scattered generously along the hundred or so yards that I could see. Everything I had read about how and where to cast seemed to swim through my head like the occasional leaf I found caught in the current. Clearly, everything I needed for good fishing was right here, and I hadn't a clue how I might proceed.

Standing hip-deep in an upstream stretch of this river I had chosen for myself, I simply cast to nowhere in particular. At first there was challenge in making the fly land where I was aiming, but before long I wanted more from my efforts. Only then did intelligible patterns begin to emerge from the crazy quilt of the river's surface. As my hand became surer in casting my fly, my eye became more practiced at picking out the likely hiding places of my quarry.

In reality, this fishing trip was conducted not on the Bighorn River but in the bowels of a university library. Standing there, hip-deep in a considerable catch of fishing literature, my mind began to parse the chaos and find patterns emerging from the depths. It occurred to me, as my bibliographic trophies began to accumulate, that I might gain some valuable insight into my topic by taking up the sport.

That was how I truly came to fly fishing. I walked into the Orvis shop, a *couple of miles down U.S. 40 from my house, looking for a handful of books. I walked out $300 poorer, but armed with a dandy fly rod and reel. I wasn't entirely sure why it was important for me to learn these skills or what I hoped to accomplish with them. But for once the furthest thing from my mind when I thought about fishing was fish.*

4

The Confluence: Roderick Haig-Brown

JUST as Frost described two roads diverging in the woods, so the wanderer among the literature of angling will eventually stand at a fork. Here, however, the roads are streams and, rather than separating, they are converging. To the left, one sees a placid chalkstream, flowing out of the Old World tradition, past the favorite haunts of the Christian apostles and Izaak Walton. The flow from that direction is considerable, but as far as one can see upstream, there is little discernible current. From the right, cascading down from higher ground, one sees the American fork, born in the misty climes frequented by the Native American and later traveled by the first Europeans to forge inland. While the stream to the right holds more immediate interest in its riffles and short cataracts, the reader knows from the map that the stream to the left is longer and, at least in pools far upriver, richer.

Unlike Frost's traveler, however, one need not choose one stream over the other in order to remain one angler. In fact, it is only at this confluence that this literary river can be called such without exaggeration. Here the calmer stream from the left is shaken and churned by the sparkling waters tumbling down from the right, forming at this junction a gently swirling pool. At the edge of this pool, nearly hidden by the overhanging willows, stands an angler, hip-deep in the combined flows that seem to have consciously created an ideal home for trout. This angler, a man, casts with the assurance of one whose hand is practiced and sure. While he gently drops his fly into the most likely-looking spots, he is at the same time never unaware of the majesty about him. The angler's name is Roderick Haig-Brown.

Haig-Brown was born on the British fork in 1908. His British roots are not only with the landed class, allowing him access to the English rivers and the fish that swam there, but also in the academy. His grandfather, William Haig-Brown, who died the year before Roderick's birth, had been not only a capable writer and scholar, but also the head of Charterhouse, one of the leading public schools in England. His father, who was killed during the First World War, had been a master at Lancing College in Sussex (Read 1981, 178–79). Roderick, in his later life, served ably in his adopted home of British Columbia as a magistrate and as chancellor of the University of Victoria (Woodcock 1981, 180).

Despite a heritage and ability that would most likely have afforded him a life in the British upper-middle class, Haig-Brown, in 1926, removed to British Columbia, where he spent most of the remainder of his life, working first as a logger, trapper, fisherman, hunter, and guide and later settling down to a life as a respectable citizen and productive writer (Read 1981, 179). It was in this remote locale that Haig-Brown married and raised his children, yet no reader can move very far into the waters that he covers in his many books without realizing that Haig-Brown in no way "went native" when he moved to the Northwest. The man fishing the pool at the junction of the two streams describes himself as Canadian, yet is very clearly British. George Woodcock, in the introduction to *Measure of the Year*, places Haig-Brown in the company of the great English nature writers:

It is this English tradition that Haig-Brown continues so nobly in *Measure of the Year,* for if one can see him as a Canadian writer by habitat and loyalty, he is equally certainly an English writer by descent and tradition. It was in England—Izaak Walton's country—that as a boy he learnt the skills of fishing on which his more popular reputation as a writer was built up. (Woodcock 1990, vii–viii)

Woodcock describes Haig-Brown as simply a transplanted Englishman—an Izaak Walton working from Vancouver Island. Such a move, however, is overly simple, akin to considering Joseph Conrad to be simply a Pole working in a foreign medium. Haig-Brown was wholly British and wholly North American at the same time. As such a hybrid, he expresses certain concerns that mark and identify the other North American writers who will follow him. In the following passage from *The Master and His Fish,* Haig-Brown sounds much more like Thoreau than like any British writer:

> Hunters and fishermen were the first explorers, and the joy of discovery has never faded in either sport. The hidden lake where the trout run big, the forgotten lagoon where the wild geese pitch, the sunken rock in the bend where the salmon lie. . . . It is not necessary to be the original discoverer, though that is perhaps the brightest pleasure of all; it is enough to feel the discovery, to have come to it by some exercise of wisdom and woodcraft, and to know that it is shared by only a few others. (1981, 82)

This passage includes the idea of frontier and first discovery that is almost completely absent from the British tradition. A biography of another English angler and writer transplanted to Canada, John Buchan, describes that writer's early fishing experiences in a manner that underscores this essential difference between the two countries:

> John Buchan developed into a hardy walker and ranged the hills in search of new burns to fish, until the ranging became an end in itself, and with his catch in his pockets he would drop down again to Broughton for tea— new-baked scones, and apple-and-rowanberry jelly—having charted yet another corner of his world, Scrape, or Broad Law, or set eyes on yet another new landmark. . . . He traced the burns to their sources, and could have drawn a map of the upper Tweed with all its tributaries accurately plotted. (Janet Smith 1965, 18)

The map that John Buchan could have accurately plotted was a map that had been capably plotted by professional cartographers for decades if not centuries before. Buchan's English world yielded the pleasures of discovering that which had been discovered countless times before, while Haig-Brown's Canada, made perhaps more dramatic after his childhood, which would have been similar to that of Buchan, holds the possibility of the new discovery, one novel not just for the discoverer but also for all people. Buchan's work, like Haig-Brown's, evolves to appreciate the wilderness and its magnitude. In *Sick Heart River*, one of Buchan's last novels, the hero, Sir Edward Leithen, who has been diagnosed with terminal tuberculosis, ventures into progressively more remote wilderness, finally dwelling among the Eskimos of far northern Canada. This wilderness possesses a healing quality for both Leithen and the mentally ill Galliard, whom Leithen had traveled to locate. The magnitude of the Arctic becomes an overwhelming presence in the novel, something that rarely, if ever, happens in the works of those who write of angling in Britain.

For Haig-Brown, the wilderness was less remote, but still vast. In the same introduction cited above, George Woodcock compares Haig-Brown to Thoreau, listing him among other "chroniclers of the country life" with Jean-Henri Fabre, the French entomologist, and Ivan Turgenev in *Sportsman's Sketches*. It may be that in seeking to make Haig-Brown a British writer, Woodcock is succumbing to the temptation to unnecessary simplification. He notes that "in England there was a notable tradition of writers about nature and the countryside, the best of whom Roderick Haig-Brown lists at one point in *Measure of the Year*, when he describes to us the library in his house" (1990, vii), yet Woodcock does not seem ready to acknowledge that this same tradition he celebrates helped to create a new and thriving tradition in the Americas. This tradition, embodied by Thoreau and Emerson, among others, is not confined to the living of an active life engaging a natural present, but expands also into a mental life, which actively engages a rich literary heritage. Haig-Brown finds no conflict in the overlap between the contemplative and active lives, going so far as to describe his library in terms of nature. "I think a library should not be a static thing but rather like a deep pool in a river, whose depths move slowly if at all but whose surface is a quiet flow" (1990, 171).

Far from seeing any conflict between the active and passive, or between his British past and Canadian present, Haig-Brown seems to find in these apparent conflicts the answer to the question of why fly fishing holds such appeal for him and others.

> Fishing is not really a simpleton's sport. It is a sport with a long history, an intricate tradition, and a great literature. These things have not grown by accident. They have developed by the devotion of sensitive and intelligent men and they make not only a foundation for rich and satisfying experience but the charter of a brotherhood that reaches around the world and through both hemispheres. (1981, 179)

Fishing is undeniably sport, yet its appeal is not located solely in its active nature or in any animalistic response. While Haig-Brown does not deny these appeals, he does not detach them from the history, the tradition, the literature, and the overall life of the mind that one sees represented in the modern fly fisher.

In addressing the question of why fishing holds its appeal, Haig-Brown does not stand in the direct lineage of the British angling writers (with the arguable exception of Luce). Instead, he reaches back to the formula practiced by Berners, Walton, and many of the other early angling writers. Before telling how one should fish, Haig-Brown joins these authors by refusing to beg the question of why one should fish. Unlike his predecessors, however, Haig-Brown does not take up the question in anything like an apologetic tone. Where Berners and Walton attempt to argue angling's superior virtues in an age when fishing was not in ascendancy, Haig-Brown instead writes in an era when fishing has far outstripped hunting and, especially, hawking, as an outdoor sport. With no need to serve as apologist, Haig-Brown takes the question as a mystery to be solved. It is not enough for him simply to fish; he must understand why fishing holds such delight for him and millions of others.

The question is considered in such great depth and in so many of his books that it cannot be ignored. Two of his four "season" books take up the question at considerable length. In the first of the four seasons, *Fisherman's Spring*, he provides perhaps the finest statement of the worthiness of fishing as a topic for serious consideration that has yet been written in English:

> The sport of fishing is an important part of life to many thousands of people, perhaps several millions of people, on this continent alone. It needs no more than this to make it an important subject. But it is also something more than a sport. It is intimate exploration of a part of the world hidden from the eyes and minds of ordinary people. It is a way of thinking and doing, a way of reviving the mind and body, that men have been following with growing intensity for hundreds of years. Fishing has contributed much to the minds of statesmen and Supreme Court justices, college presidents and philosophers, auto workers, pulp mill workers . . . ; in turn, they and many others have contributed to the sport until it has become an art, ephemeral, graceful, complicated, full of tradition, yet never static. It is as much a part of modern civilization as most of the minor arts and sciences and probably has more direct effect on more lives than any of them. (1975b, 10–11)

The third book of the seasonal tetralogy, *Fisherman's Summer*, traces the evolution of a reflective angler, detailing how he came to find in fishing something that most people cannot see. In his youth, Haig-Brown says, he felt that fishing was "a simple contest between man and fish." He took credit for the good fishing that he had, blaming the bad fishing on luck (1975c, 246). "But I am beginning to find it very salutary to remember just how much 'happening right,' if not downright luck, there has been in nearly all my little triumphs. Often there has been so little between success and failure that I feel little inclined to take much credit unless for perseverance" (247).

While he touches on the question in the seasonal books, he delves fully into it in other writings. "Why do we pursue these fish so hard?" Haig-Brown asks in *The Master and His Fish*. He suggests as possible answers the desire to capture impressive trophies, the attraction of travel to a great fishing river, the intricacies and craftsmanship of fine fishing gear, or the marvels to be found in the birds, plants, animals, and landscapes that form the surroundings of those great rivers. These answers he concedes are valid ones, yet they do not seem sufficient in his mind. "But there is nearly always something else, too, more subtle and more complicated. We are hoping to create or recreate some ideal situation" (1981, 17). One can scarcely read these sentences without thinking of Nick Adams attempting to recapture his youthful fishing experiences on the Big Two-Hearted River, yet Haig-Brown is describing something that is potentially much simpler. That ideal situation he describes is a personal creation. For him, the ideal was bringing a rise out of a trout on a chalkstream in the south of England. "[T]he ideal was in the scene and in the action up to the setting of the hook. What happened afterwards in those weed-choked streams was often anticlimactic and even a little untidy" (ibid.). In *Fisherman's Summer*, Haig-Brown ascribes virtually the same ideal situation to one of Britain's legendary anglers. "To Frederick Halford, good fishing was the taking of wise, feeding brown trout on a surface fly that matched the natural and so brought triumph through complete deception" (1975c, 251). This same sentiment is expressed by Howell Raines's fishing companion, Dick Blalock: "I finally decided that the fun was not in landing the fish. The fun was in seeing the fish take. So I began cutting my Sculpins right at the bend of the hook, and they would grab it, and I would jerk it out of their mouth" (Raines 1994, 156).

The British tradition, as it had evolved in the early years of this century, assumed that the "why" question was self-evident: one fishes in order to land and consume fish. Haig-Brown, however, sees the question as not only not self-evident, but not capable of answer except at the personal level. The fish-quest is not so much an effort to connect with the trout, but an effort to connect with something within the angler: "So we search for trout in many ways and many places, each of us, I suspect, with some secret inward vision, subconscious as often as not, of what trout fishing really is" (1981, 21). Later in the same work, he expresses again the element of self-discovery in fishing: "It is a sport that can never grow old. We follow the traditions, but do not hesitate to bend and twist them to our needs. We dream dreams and make plans and nearly always fail in the execution of them. We surprise ourselves often, perhaps because we know so little about it all, perhaps because we are such simple souls" (24).

It is important to remember that Haig-Brown, while not oversubscribing to the traditional reasons for fishing, does not dismiss them. In the following passage, he sums up his attitude toward the sport:

> This is what fishing is all about. Not just repeating over and over the things one knows can be done. Not just catching and killing. Not battling monsters of incredible strength and fury—the odds, after all, are nearly always with the fisherman. Not even in enduring harsh weather conditions. It is in developing and refining knowledge of the fish themselves that show them at their best. . . . The challenge is not: "Can you catch him?" It is rather: "Can you catch him in the way you want, with fullest respect for his qualities and a real testing of your own skills?" It is a fascinating challenge and one that never grows old. (1981, 97)

Haig-Brown does not downplay the catch or the battle, but neither does he overplay these aspects of the sport. The real heart of fishing, for him, is a battle of wits, but it is not that between fish and angler. Instead, Haig-Brown engages himself in that battle. Ironically, it is in a land of plenty that he moves toward a qualitative position, while his British forebears, in a land of very limited fishing resources, focused largely on the quantitative aspect of the sport.

Not only does Haig-Brown stand at the confluence of the two major traditions in fly-fishing literature, but he also can be best described as standing astride lines of division. His work, although still in print and considerable, seems to defy categorization. Unlike Hemingway's or Norman Maclean's, Haig-Brown's writings do not fit neatly enough into the traditional literary genres to have warranted any significant critical attention. The MLA Bibliography reveals only one article (in reality a strange combination of three brief reviews by different authors) published about Haig-Brown in literary journals. While apparently not belonging to the literary tradition of angling writing (or at least not occupying a terribly significant place in that tradition), this body of work also seems to fall short of the mark as instructive literature. Haig-Brown does not instruct the reader on how to tie flies or match the hatch. His paintings of rivers are much more apt to be created with a broad and impressionistic brush than are those of such writers as Ernest Schwiebert or Datus Proper. In fact, at times it might be surmised that Haig-Brown does not really know all that much of the technical side of fishing. At the beginning of *Fisherman's Spring,* he begins with an apology that he likens to that affixed by Milton to the beginning of *Lycidas.* "Certainly I am not impressed with myself when I read the books of other fishermen and realize what effort and devotion they spend on their experiments and research and on just plain fishing" (1975b, 9). In the course of his books, he is much more apt than the more technical angling writers to leave the stream altogether, spending a portion of *Fisherman's Spring* discussing the identification of birds, describing in *Fisherman's Summer* the Indian and early explorers who traveled his woods in the past, or ranging into the care of livestock or the building of a library in *Measure of the Year.* Despite these dalliances, the gurgles of the waters of the stream are always to be heard in the background of his work. In *Fisherman's Spring,* Haig-Brown calls himself "a writer first and a fisherman second" (9), yet this does not seem to explain the balance completely. In reviewing his work, it seems more accurate to describe him as a fully wrought human, for whom angling is an important part of life. Angling and the proximity of a river are facets of his life that he clearly treasures; however, they are no more important than other facets such as writing, reading, family, civic duty, and farming. The potential for Haig-Brown's reputation in either the literary world or the technical fly-fishing world was perhaps stunted by this balance, yet those who travel his quiet waters find him to be worthwhile.

While not read for the latest technical information nor placed in the canon of mainstream literature, Haig-Brown has, without question, created a place for himself in the pantheon of North American fly fishing. A number of examples will help to explain this niche. The Federation of Fly Fishers presents an annual award for "significant contributions to angling literature." The award is named for Roderick Haig-Brown. In the preface to Steve Raymond's *The Year of the Angler,* Arnold Gingrich writes, "Enos

Bradner, Roderick Haig-Brown, Ben Hur Lampman . . . so begins the roll-call of Legend, as subject of Western fishing comes up" (1995, 9). David James Duncan offers an unlikely homage from a horrific visage on the Deschutes River: "It stands six-foot-six in hip boots, weighs 240 flabless pounds, has flaming read hair and huge red hands and is prone to sudden outbursts of violence. Its name is Jeremiah Ransom" (1995, 163). When Jeremiah is greeted by name by an angler for whom he has nothing but contempt, Ransom replies, "I'm Roderick Haig-Brown" (175–76). Ransom could hardly have chosen a more storied figure or one less like himself.

Clearly, Haig-Brown has established himself as a major figure in the waters of American fly fishing, yet as noted above, he does not do so, as have some, on the strengths of his angling expertise. Like Ben Hur Lampman, Haig-Brown made his chief contribution to his sport not in his ability to cast a fly but in his ability to cast a sentence. Clearly, the man could write with both accuracy and grace, as this passage from *The Master and His Fish* demonstrates:

> Fish such as black bass, Atlantic salmon, dorado, bonefish, striped bass, muskies, tarpon, pickerel, or what have you, may be local fishermen's favourites. But for universal popularity and world-wide distribution there is no other fish to compare with the trouts. Trout are practically synonymous with angling, and there are few anglers who do not try for them sooner or later. Many will fish for nothing else during their entire angling lives, and most of these enthusiasts will go as far as funds and time will let them in search of trout fishing that is better or perhaps merely different in some small way from any they have known. If a trout fisherman must stay for a long time in a land where there are no trout, he will almost inevitably look into ways of introducing them; and as often as not he will find some way. . . . There are many obvious reasons for the trouts' popularity. Trout are very elegant creatures, clean and graceful in form, usually handsome or even beautiful in colouration. They are vigorous and active in performance, prompt and hearty feeders, and a delicacy on the table. They frequent, by preference, pleasant and beautiful places. . . . They learn quickly to beware of the shadow of man and all the delicate devices he creates for their deception. This naturally leads man on to further extravagances of cunning and ingenuity and so keeps the whole thing going. (1981, 12–13)

This is fine writing, but it hardly outshines the product of many fine journalists in any age. In no way can Haig-Brown's prose style alone account for his enduring position in the sport and its literature. What does perhaps help to account for this position is the unique view of the sport that he presented to his readers. Fishing, for Haig-Brown, is anything but a simple thing. He does not set out in the morning simply to pluck trout from a stream. Instead, he goes to the river in order to attempt a meaning-making activity. In fact, if one were to substitute words relating to reading and literature for those relating to fishing and nature, certain of Haig-Brown's passages could be added to a literature-class textbook with little or no further editing. One such passage can be found in *Fisherman's Spring*:

> This book has no message. . . . But it has in large measure grown from the intimate, relaxed exploration of the wood that seems to me the highest satisfaction this most sophisticated of sports can offer. Its intention is only to share pleasure as fishermen share a joke or a fly or a flask beside a stream. The writing of it has been pleasure and in itself often a deeper exploration of the hidden places of the wood. I know well that there are other ways through, from daylight to daylight, than my own, other treasures to search for than those I seek. One of the charms of the sport is its infinite complexity, its scope for men of diverse minds and bodies and skills. The pattern of discovery may vary widely; that does not matter. The important thing is that the wood has depth and richness to reward a lifetime of quiet, perceptive searching. (1975b, 221–22)

In *Fisherman's Fall*, he again celebrates both the tradition of fishing and its potential for creative action: "Fishing is not a sport I expect ever to exhaust or abandon. It has led me and still leads me into too many delights for that. Yet there are times now when I find myself wondering just what it is I am going out to find, with the familiar tackle, in the familiar water at a time made familiar by many past seasons. Is it reasonable to expect some new experience?" (1975a, 209). This dual appreciation for tradition and the creation of new tradition is expressed early in *Fisherman's Spring*: "The sport as we now have it is at something approaching full flower, technically as perfect as it needs to be, but still open to infinite creative interpretation. Its future is in the hands of the enormous numbers of men and women who now have leisure and opportunity to pursue it. They have to carry it into a new phase that will somehow combine protective limitations with the expansive ideas of a new continent" (1975b, 12).

In writing of fly patterns, Haig-Brown again champions the creative aspect of his sport. He eschews the strict imitation of insects, suggesting that while sometimes imitation brings rewards, perhaps more often, straying from the orthodox brings bigger rewards. In fact, he suggests, some deviances from the orthodox have become so well known as to form a new orthodoxy (1981, 169).

While the constant validation of creative aspects of the sport are hallmarks of Haig-Brown's work, from beginning to end, his appreciation of that which has gone before is equally evident. Not only, as evidenced several times above, does he value the legacy of those who developed the sport in centuries past, but he also appreciates the larger world of human existence, of which fishing is a part. Unlike the narrator of David James Duncan's *The River Why*, for whom fishing is the beginning and end and for whom *The Compleat Angler* was the only significant book, Haig-Brown, in describing the building of a library, scarcely mentions the literature of angling, championing instead

> Chaucer, Malory, Bacon, Shakespeare, Donne, Burton; lively Herrick, gentle Walton, giant Milton; the diarists, then Crashaw, Hooker, Defoe, Swift, Addison, Steele, and Pope. So to the first novelists, Richardson, Fielding, Sterne, Smollett. Between Smollett and Jane Austen, at the end of the first section, there is a diversity of giants: Adam Smith, Gibbon, Dr. Johnson, Cobbet of the Rural Rides, Blake and Burns before him, Wordsworth, Scott, and Coleridge after. (1990, 167)

Besides his appreciation for the culture that made his rich life possible, Haig-Brown also has a deep reverence for the natural world in which his sport takes place. It is a commonplace of angling writing to note the beauty of rivers in which trout live, to anthropomorphize the fish, or to blithely admire nature's wonders, but Haig-Brown's feelings transcend any connection to fishing. He does not love rivers because he loves fishing. Quite the contrary, he loves fishing because to do so is a natural outgrowth of his love for the rivers in which the fish exist. In *Measure of the Year*, he overtly states his passion for rivers: "I think it is a natural thing for a man to love a river, and I think I should still want to live by one if I had never caught a fish or fired a gun. A river is life and light, especially in timbered country. . . . No clean river can be other than beautiful and it has changing beauty" (1990, 253). Later in the same chapter, he further details his attitude toward the river, underscoring the integral position of the river in his existence:

> I call the river mine, without owning any foot of it from source to sea and without any thought of possession in the ordinary sense. At one time or another I have walked most of the valley's length; I have traveled a good part of it by boat and canoe; I have waded most places where wading is possible and the fishing makes it worthwhile. I have blazed trees at the level of highest flood and have studied the depressions and hidden rocks of the bottom in lowest summer water. . . . In all this there is an intimacy akin to possession and far more important than possession. I do not want possession, only freedom of the river; and with every growth of knowledge and experience freedom grows. . . . If one had to live out a life whose sight was limited to the breadth of the river at one place, the full measure of the year and all the seasons would be in it, as plainly there as in the pages of the handsomest calendar ever drawn. It would be a record of contrasts and mergence. (1990, 255–59)

Not only does Haig-Brown call the river his, but it would not be extreme, after reading these passages, to say that he is the river's. He lived the majority of his life, as nearly as a human might, on the river—his house built "rather over a hundred feet from the edge of the river" (1990, 8)—and the river is as surely a part of his circulatory system as the veins that carry his blood.

For Haig-Brown, fishing is not simply the pursuit of fish. In several places he laments the many anglers who pursue fish but do not enjoy the transcendent quality that he finds in the sport. In *The Master and His Fish*, he observes that of the millions of anglers who fish every year, "there isn't a reason in the world to suppose that [they all] really enjoy going fishing; a remarkably high proportion of them contribute vastly to the discomfort of others while finding little joy in the sport for themselves" (1981, 179). While the joyless anglers may enjoy all of the best tackle and physical ability that the technical writers recommend, their type of angling lacks in emotional depth. In Haig-Brown's opinion, it is not enough simply to catch fish. "The fisherman is seeking to catch fish on his own terms, terms that will yield him the greatest sense of achievement and the closest identification with his quarry" (1981, 180). He goes on to suggest that success in angling is not directly related to the size of the catch. "It is just possible that nice guys don't catch the most fish. But they find far more pleasure in those they do get" (184).

As an angler who came of age on the chalkstreams of England in the time of Frederic Halford and Bliss Perry, this renunciation of the catch as the ultimate object of the angler is perhaps the most surprising thing one finds in the pages that Haig-Brown has left. His legacy is the simple yet profound realization that "it is enough simply to go fishing. The rest is bound to follow. . . . The object is to go fishing, to enjoy going fishing and perhaps to perform well enough to solve a few problems and catch a few fish. An assortment of miracles achieved by gadgets out of *Popular Mechanics* would be enough to upset the whole business" (1981, 219).

While the balance between tradition and innovation, the Thoreau-like desire to become part of the natural world, and the subordination of the catch to other aspects of angling all make Haig-Brown significant, it is difficult to say if any one or a combination of these is the element that has helped his work to endure over the past half century. It is perhaps because the essential quality of Haig-Brown's writing is so difficult to fix with any certainty that he has been so ignored by critics. This study does not pretend to have ascertained the precise locus of his genius or the reason for his enduring appeal. Despite this shortcoming, two pieces of atypical Haig-Brown writing may be used in contrast to better see the value in the typical.

The first of these examples comes from *Fisherman's Winter*, the third of the seasons series to be published. Rather than writing, as he had before, of his adopted home of British Columbia, Haig-Brown presents his winter volume as more of an enthusiastic travelogue for South American fly fishing. Having been commissioned to visit Chile and Argentina in order to assist in the development of sporting tourism, Haig-Brown clearly enjoyed his travels, presenting them in an uncritical manner, much more focused on the water and much less on the surrounding flora, fauna, and landscape than the accounts in the previous books. Where, in *Measure of the Year*, Haig-Brown talks of his deep knowledge of Vancouver Island's Elk River, one gets the feeling in his winter study that his enthusiasm and the lack of his usual perspective might derive from the shallowness of his acquaintance with these southern rivers.

A second bit of atypical prose is considerably shorter. In *Fisherman's Fall*, the last of the seasons books to be published, he dedicates several late chapters to a discussion of both his enthusiasm for and his misgivings regarding scuba diving as a means of reconnaissance. This is a curious section of the book since it sheds light on the more traditional fishing sections of the text by way of its marked contrast. It is clear to the reader that Haig-Brown has become enamored of scuba just as many of its participants do. His enthusiasm for this sport is really no different from his enthusiasm for fly fishing, although his zeal is somewhat fresher and less settled in the former than in the latter (1975a, 273–79).

What is lacking from these two examples of the Haig-Brown legacy is at least part of what makes the remainder so worthwhile. Typically, Roderick Haig-Brown does not dazzle the reader with either philosophical pyrotechnics or angling instruction. Instead, the reader enjoys the warmth of reading words emanating from an active and wide-ranging mind. Haig-Brown can perhaps best be described in comparison with the pool he was described as fishing at the outset of these pages. Not as immediately engaging as the riffles upstream, his work proves, after patient consideration, ultimately to be more complex and worthy of the angler's attention, and when the fishing is over or at a lull, the reader also finds that he can range over many and varied topics. Fishing, for Haig-Brown, is simply an axis or a still point. In the first of the seasons books, *Fisherman's Spring*, he describes his own attitude quite admirably:

I feel at ease with fishing, even with writing about it, because I have been through and come out on the other side. I do not mean by this that I know all the answers, or even a major fraction of them. Rather, it is as though I had found my way clear through a deep and beautiful wood, from open daylight to open daylight, and knowing the way, were free to turn back into the wood and search in peace and leisure for all its beauties. In reaching the other side I have found nothing that cannot be found without going clear through, except that the wood has a limit in at least one direction, that it is good all through and that nothing beyond seems better. (217)

As the fisherman in the pool where the forks meet throws his hands back, bending his nine-foot pole into an arching parabola, the observer would do well to study his actions. They will be repeated, although with variety, at many points downstream. Just as the anglers who will follow Haig-Brown will employ the same four-count rhythm in their casting, they will also explore their world with a similar four-point perspective. They, like Haig-Brown, will assiduously take up the question of why one fishes and particularly why one fly fishes. They will explore the question of how one should fish. They will study the relations between fishing and the broader world, and they will look downstream to see the impact that their sport and their lives will leave upon the waters.

Interlude 4

First Casts

I MADE my way to the Orvis store that day with innocent pursuits in mind. Not really. I told myself and my wife and anyone else who cared to listen that I was going to look for a book. The exact title escapes me now. But deep down I knew what I was really going for, something nine feet long and not remotely similar to a book. I walked out of the store with a fine fly rod. It even had a twenty-five-year warranty.

"Even if you slam the trunk lid on it and break it, Orvis will replace it for free," the clerk had assured me.

I took that as an omen and laid the Visa card on the counter.

My first tentative attempts at casting took place in the front of the house. The street was my river and the garage door was the backcast hazard that I would soon know all too well. By the time I could, with some semblance of grace, drop the single fly that the Orvis lady had given me into my neighbor's driveway, I deemed myself ready to fish.

As luck would provide, I was accompanying the family to a church retreat for the weekend. Before the Orvis trip, I hadn't been in the least enthusiastic about this little jaunt, but given that the camp sported two lightly fished lakes and plenty of room for a hack fly caster to make mistakes, I became the zealous maniac, urging everyone to load the car faster on Friday evening.

Mostly due to my insistence, we reached the lovely shores of Lake Doniphan a couple of hours ahead of sunset. After dumping all the gear that we brought for the weekend, I assembled my rod and clambered to the marshy lakeside. I learned several valuable things that weekend. First, as I made my way through the camp lodge, I came to realize why fly rods could be broken down into smaller pieces. Second, I learned that you always need at least one more leader than you bring with you. Third, I found how hard it was to cast in the wind.

The wind that evening was stiff. No matter where I aimed my cast, the fly went plunking into the water directly to my right. I had no idea how well I was doing. If this were not bad enough, a scruffy-looking lad walked my way as soon as the first cast hit the water.

"Are you fly fishing?" he asked, scratching himself frantically.

I wasn't entirely sure that an affirmative answer wouldn't be a lie, so I mumbled a quick "Yep."

"My dad's fishing," he added.

"Great," I answered, hoping that the kid would take the hint and wander on.

"You caught anything?"

By this time, the wind had thrown my fly into a shore-hugging patch of the gooiest algae I had ever seen. "Yeah, I caught one big one. It was your size and it sure made a lot of noise."

He laughed, but clearly didn't catch the reference. "That's a good one." He wiped his nose on his shirt sleeve. "You want to fish with my dad?"

I imagined what I would like to say to the kid. "Sure, I'd like nothing more than to look like a fool in front of a stranger," but I held it in. Maybe ignoring him was the answer.

"My dad fishes here a lot." He continued when I didn't answer. "Do you fish here a lot?"

"No, I sure don't," I said, cursing under my breath as the wind tossed my fly completely away from the water and into the grass. Maybe ignoring him and really heaving on the old rod was the answer.

"Yeah, I like coming here when my dad fishes."

Should you be in a similar situation—two pieces of advice. First, do not become so frustrated that you grab the kid and toss him into the lake. That would be wrong. Second, do not become so frustrated that you think really heaving on the old rod is the answer. That, perhaps, would be even more wrong.

When I looked at the end of the rod, I found that an amazingly complex knot had been tied out of my leader by unseen hands. Loop after loop of monofilament wrapped and coiled around the rod. My fly hung by about four inches of free line.

"Did you get a tangle?" the kid asked.

Remember, do not throw the kid in the lake. "Yeah, I sure did," I said as calmly as I could. "Guess I'll have to call it a night." I gathered my possessions and headed back to the lodge.

"Okay," he called after me. "Are you going to fish tomorrow?"

I drew a deep breath and, without turning, answered. "Probably."

He was smiling. I could see it without turning around. "Great. I guess I'll see you tomorrow then."

Small mercies do come about sometimes, however. I did indeed fish the next day and the kid never made an appearance. Neither did the wind, I should add. It was a perfect day to fish, so I did.

It was probably no more than my third or fourth cast that drew an explosive strike. The flash of tail and the power of the initial hit identified the largemouth bass. I swept my rod back and set the hook in a heartbeat. A few moments later, the fish was ashore, twenty inches of quivering scales and fins.

I had scarcely had time to fix him onto my stringer and get the line back into the water when a second fish blasted out of the water with my line trailing from his mouth. This one, although a fraction smaller than the first, made a more determined fight of things, running behind a fallen log before succumbing to my reel.

Another fish, nearly the size of the first, came along a few minutes later, and then, after twenty minutes or so of fruitless prospecting led me down the shore a hundred yards or so, three more arrived in rapid succession. My stringer looked like the one that Andy and Opie carry along at the end of the old Andy Griffith Show, and I carried it with pride back to the lodge and my family. It was, with little doubt, the best fishing day of my life.

I could end there, but that wouldn't be entirely honest. I have not exaggerated about the fish, their sizes, or their number, but I might have allowed you to assume that my Orvis flyrod was somehow involved in the transaction. In truth, after the fiasco of the previous night, I had packed away the flyrod and broken out my trusty spinning rig. A Texas-rigged plastic worm had dredged those bass out of their beds. I was still a fly-fishing virgin.

5

Big Two-Hearted Writer: Part One

DOWNSTREAM from Roderick Haig-Brown the quiet pool at the confluence of the two forks quickly gives way to a loud and tumultuous run of water where stands another fisherman. This figure can hardly be ignored for he bestrides the stream like a colossus. The literature of fly fishing might be taken as a mere backwater eddy to the overall current of American literature if it were not for the importance of fishing in the work of one of the most important figures in that canon, Ernest Hemingway.

Unlike Haig-Brown, for whom fishing was simply a natural part of a full life, Hemingway seemed to embrace fishing as something more. Fishing, like writing, for Hemingway was a simple act of nature and at the same time something immensely more significant. Both facets of his life, tied together as they were, were simultaneously literal and figurative. One critic suggests that "fishing stories were the alpha and omega of his career. 'Big Two-Hearted River,' written in 1924 while he was in Europe, was the first of his writings to become well known. It marked his debut into American literature. The novel *The Old Man and the Sea*, written in Cuba in 1951, won him the Nobel Prize. It was the last major work of his lifetime" (Lawrence 1992, 8).

For Hemingway, fishing—fly and otherwise—was an important component in the mythos that he forged for himself; however, despite the legendary quality of the author's life or his pastimes, it cannot be denied that fishing held a special place in the private man as well. This private significance reveals itself in several places, including in several of the short stories, most notably "Big Two-Hearted River," and in three novels, *The Sun Also Rises*, *The Old Man and the Sea*, and *Islands in the Stream*. In "Big Two-Hearted River" and *The Sun Also Rises*, the fishing is fly fishing and thus central to the study at hand. In the other, later novels, the fishing is deep-sea fishing and related for the attitudes toward the sport but not the technique. Gregory Sojka places fishing in a position of primacy for the understanding of Hemingway, arguing that Hemingway's "personal statements and fictional uses elevate fishing beyond a mere sport of leisure activity to an important exercise in ordering and reinforcing an entire philosophy and style of life" (1985, xi).

Before proceeding to an examination of the fictional works dealing with fly fishing, it is worthwhile to pause for a moment on a piece of Hemingway's journalistic output, which appeared before any of the fiction to be considered below. The story "The Best Rainbow Trout Fishing" first appeared on August 28, 1920, when Hemingway was only twenty-one, in the *Toronto Star Weekly*, where it might easily have disappeared from publication in anything but the most thorough compendium of Hemingway's work had it not been recently reprinted in Leonard M. Wright's curious collection *The Fly Fisher's Reader*. The story is a straightforward celebration of excellent fishing. At first glance, nothing in the piece seems to indicate that Hemingway approaches fishing as anything more significant than catching fish, as seen in this passage:

There [on the Canadian Soo river] the rainbow have been taken as large as fourteen pounds from canoes that are guided through the rapids and halted at the pools by Ojibway and Chippewa boatmen. It is a wild and nerve-frazzling sport and the odds are in the favor of the big trout who tear off thirty or forty yards of line at a rush and then will sulk at the base of a big rock and refuse to be stirred into action by the pumping of a stout fly rod aided by a fluent monologue of Ojibwayian profanity. (205)

In the following paragraph, however, Hemingway casts two short, declarative sentences that begin to suggest the more profound things to come: "The Soo affords great fishing. But it is a wild nightmare kind of fishing" (205). Here is fishing of a divided nature. The fishing is great, but is at the same time nightmarish, hardly a likely combination. Fishing, for Hemingway, is a human activity where life and death meet and stare at each other. Like the biblical fish stories and the accounts of Walton that serve as precursors for Hemingway's work, what seems on the surface to be simply a tale of human against nature belies a tremendously deeper significance.

The first of Hemingway's fishing-related fictional works to appear were the Nick Adams short stories. "Big Two-Hearted River," described as perhaps "the most analyzed—or overanalyzed—short story of our time" (Lawrence 1992, 5), is the one most completely dedicated to fly fishing and thus the one most easily approached on those terms. Hemingway placed extra stress on the importance of "Big Two-Hearted River" as the culminating story for In Our Time, not only by placing the story at the end of the collection but also by dividing it into two parts and listing each part in the table of contents, accentuating this division further by inserting an interchapter between the two parts. "Big Two-Hearted River" stands out also not only as the longest of the Nick stories, but also as a unique specimen in that it is almost wholly descriptive and includes only a single human character. Perhaps because of these unique qualities and the story's importance to Hemingway's project in In Our Time, "Big Two-Hearted River" has garnered more critical attention than any other story in the volume and more than all but two or three pieces in Hemingway's total short fiction output.

Joseph Flora, in his study of the Nick Adams stories, becomes an enthusiastic proponent of this story as a pinnacle of Hemingway's early art. Flora suggests that in the story Hemingway "was trying to do in fiction what had not been done before, and he knew he was succeeding. In 'Big Two-Hearted River' his hero was also dealing, more meaningfully than he had ever done before, with the issues of life and death—as was Joyce's Gabriel Conroy in 'The Dead'" (Flora 1982, 147).

In considering the story in terms of paradox and dividedness, one can grow just as enthusiastic, starting from some of the rather mundane facts already mentioned. As noted above, "Big Two-Hearted River" is the only story that Hemingway formally partitioned into multiple parts. One might suggest that the story's length was the cause for its division, yet Hemingway does not seem inclined to fragmentation for the sake of symmetry. Indeed, the theme of division is only begun in the literal division of the text.

Between the two parts of "Big Two-Hearted River" Hemingway places the vignette of a hanging in which a somewhat uninterested priest admonishes the condemned man, who is too weakened by fear to stand on the gallows, by saying, "Be a man, my son." At once the priest refers to the condemned man as a child, "my son," while urging him to behave as an adult. In the two halves of the story, Nick is similarly divided as to his level of maturity. His experience as an adult has left him so scarred that he feels the need to return to this place of childhood memories in order to be reborn. As Bliss Perry puts it,

> To revisit a river is like trying to redream a dream. You are aware, of
> course, that you have changed and that the river must have changed and
> that no two dreams are precisely alike. Yet the identities are more profound than the differences, and the moment you are on the stream you
> have the old illusion of timelessness. This mortal has put on immortality.
> (1927, 63)

If Nick's journey seems like a dream revisited, it may be because the reader cannot be altogether certain that it is not a waking dream that is being described rather than real life. In the other story from *In Our Time* dealing prominently with fly fishing, "Now I Lay Me," Nick describes the manner in which he passed the time in the hospital after his wounding in battle. Because he had convinced himself that if he were to sleep he would die, Nick devised a number of methods to occupy the night. The first method, and the most thoroughly described, was to

> think of a trout stream I had fished along when I was a boy and fish its whole length very carefully in my mind; fishing very carefully under all the logs, all the turns of the bank, the deep holes and the clear shallow stretches, sometimes catching trout and sometimes losing them. I would stop fishing sometimes on a high bank under a tree, and I always ate my lunch very slowly and watched the stream below me while I ate. (218–19)

The description of Nick's fishing, in all its variety, continues for two pages, including such details that appear in "Big Two-Hearted River" as catching grasshoppers, releasing them into the water, and watching a fish rise to the meal. One particularly significant echo of the later story comes as Nick describes creating new rivers in his mind: "Some of those streams I still remember and think that I have fished in them, and they are confused with streams I really know. I gave them all names and went to them on the train and sometimes walked for miles to get to them" (221).

Numerous biographical critics of Hemingway have noted that there is no *Big* Two-Hearted River in Michigan's upper peninsula. The river described in "Big Two-Hearted River" almost certainly was not the Two-Hearted River that does flow in that country but the Fox River. H. Lea Lawrence, in his book retracing Hemingway's fishing haunts, feels certain not only that the Fox was the river in question but that Nick "camped about a quarter-mile off the road near where the Big Fox and Little Fox forks meet" (1992, 4). While this may be true, Lawrence and others might be missing the point if one reads "Big Two-Hearted River" with "Now I Lay Me" in mind. "Big Two-Hearted River" might be, as most readers have assumed, a literal description of a literal fishing expedition, but, given the hints laid down in "Now I Lay Me," there exists an equal possibility that the river is a creation of Nick's mind, combined out of memories of the Fox and the name of the Two-Hearted. In such a case, the story takes place not in Michigan but in a field hospital a few miles from the lines of battle where Nick had been wounded.

While the very epistemic reality of the narration can be questioned, division can be found also in a considerably more prosaic site: at the textual boundaries of the story. The last paragraph of the story reverses the first. In the first, the reader is told that "Nick sat down." At the end, "Nick stood up," apparently embracing life and action. Although properly called a fishing story, the text spends as much time dealing with nonfishing matters as with the actual fishing. Flora suggests that the "fishing is not everything; the getting to the place of the fishing is as worthy of our attention as is the fishing action of Part II" (1982, 158), pointing out the essential division of the story, with part one consisting of getting to the camp and part two consisting of venturing out from the camp.

The story's doubleness is also represented in the words of the title. First, the word *Big* suggests that a Little Two-Hearted River is also to be found in those environs. Probably more significantly, the other name of the river, Two-Hearted, is ambiguous in the extreme. It might be read as indicating duplicitousness, with both its sunny shallows in which the trout swim and the forbidding, dark swamp that Nick is not yet ready to fish. In this sense the river, like life, is kind and providential at one moment only to turn cruel and destructive at the next. On the other hand, the term *two-hearted* could be read to denote the hope of rebirth. This river is one that Nick has fished in his childhood. Having given Nick "heart" once in his childhood, the river might provide for him once again in this time of need. In this sense, "two-hearted" might almost be seen as a question. Nick knows that the river had one heart to give him, but does it have another? A final way in which the title might be read is as "double-minded." Certainly Nick comes to the river as a divided psyche. His comments as he travels the countryside, the deliberateness with which he establishes his camp and cooks his meals, suggests that he is preoccupied and probably barely maintaining control of his emotions. Several times in "Big Two-Hearted River" Hemingway tells us that Nick is happy, yet various actions —his nervous reaction to the first hooking of a fish, his smoking—indicate the underlying tautness of his nerves.

Just as the textual elements of the story emphasize dividedness and paradox, so do some of the images that Hemingway employs in telling the story, beginning with the river that is the center of the story. One writer notes that "the river as symbol implies the possibility of revitalization at one extreme but absolute destruction at the other" (DeFalco 1963, 148), yet the river as literal is just as capable of expressing oppositions. Rivers, by their very nature, are dividing entities, branching upward into myriad tiny portions of the watershed.

Underlying the text of this story, yet strangely silent, is the overall theme of the collection of stories and the historical event that unifies it: World War I. As Flora points out, the story "is about the trauma of war, although the story never mentions the war" (1982, 147). The river can be likened to the war in some ways. "The Big Two-Hearted river is the river of life and death, and each implies the other. In terms of the image of the very first day that Hemingway has built upon, it is the river of both morning and evening. The joy of morning implies the journey to the darker shadows" (173). The swamp, even as it frightens Nick away at the close of the story, seems to draw him to it.

For Joseph Flora, the war is an irrepressible force from the past, constantly and wickedly attempting to impinge on Nick's present. He supports this idea by describing Nick's early-morning fishing action. Nick watches the first grasshopper that he attempts to hook sucked into the current of the river and then eaten by a trout. He baits his hook with the second grasshopper. "Although he is killing the hopper, he respects the hopper's life. Nick has a sense of communion with the creatures different only in degrees, not kind, from what Santiago will later demonstrate in *The Old Man and the Sea* when he kills the marlin. Nick in looking at the first hopper has seen the rhythm of the Big Two-Hearted River—the rhythm of life and death. War is a violation of this sacred rhythm" (Flora 1982, 168). What Flora seems not to realize is that the rhythm of war and the rhythm of life and death are not two different and irreconcilable rhythms, but instead, to use his words, "different only in degrees, not kind" (168). The rhythm of war is loud and overwhelming, but its cadence is the same that is found here in the waters of the Big Two-Hearted River, and if Nick can become complacent standing in the open water, he must nevertheless always realize, if only in the back of his mind, that the swamp exists downstream.

Flora compares this action with "Stopping by Woods on a Snowy Evening" (174), but it might just as well be compared to *The Red Badge of Courage* or the poetry of Wilfred Owen. In Crane's work, the war begins as a glorious romance, decays quickly into a miasma of terror, but finally resolves into something terrible but tolerable. Even in the decidedly antiwar poems of Wilfred Owen, the horror of war is something irresistible and compelling. There is life and opportunity in the death and destruction of war, just as there is the shadow of the swamp in the light of the river. The fact that the war's horror is not mentioned does not make it less tangible; like yin and yang, Hemingway suggests that the presence of one of the terms of these equations—light and dark, life and death, hope and despair—evokes the absent one just as well as that term's presence might do.

Another facet of doubleness or paradox in this story and in many of Hemingway's stories is implied in the foregoing observation. For Hemingway, the most powerful element of the text, in many cases, was that which was not present. In *A Moveable Feast*, Hemingway discusses the idea of omission: "you could omit anything if you knew that you omitted it and the omitted part would strengthen the story and make people feel something more than they understood." (1964, 75) One critic explains the artist's decision as follows: "It was the tension Hemingway valued, not the Thing that caused the tension, so he left the Thing out" (Julian Smith 1970–71, 169). Tension, of course, requires two or more forces operating more or less in opposition, an idea that might seem to be simply another way of expressing the literary idea of conflict. Conflict, however, suggests resolution, while tension suggests continuation. This is what Hemingway valued in this story and in *The Sun Also Rises*. It is the dividedness and the tension that this state of doubleness produces that defines the world that the author creates.

With Hemingway's idea of omission in mind, one can attempt to understand the appeal of the story. "Every sentence of this story seems to sound a harmonic of larger and parallel meaning, as if it were in code. And the key is the river, the stream of consciousness, of time, of life. Fishing, as later in *The Old Man and the Sea*, becomes something ritualistic, something symbolic of larger endeavor" (Baker 1975, 153). While nothing of import seems to happen in "Big Two-Hearted River," the reader nevertheless finds the tale engrossing. There is, perhaps as Sheridan Baker suggests, something larger going on behind the scenes, some sort of magic.

The one aspect of this story in which the idea of dividedness seems to break down is in its dramatis personae. Despite the prominence of doubleness, this is the only story in which Nick or any of Hemingway's characters is absolutely alone. Even Santiago in *The Old Man and the Sea* begins and ends his adventure in the company of others. For all the reader knows, Nick is the only human being on the face of the earth and the blackened earth he encounters early in the story is the aftermath of nuclear holocaust. Nick's solitude, is not, however, a violation of the strong trend toward dividedness in the story. Nick is alone, yet as he looks down from the bridge at the trout, the fish turn into more than the objects of his sport—"they are, in terms of Santiago of *The Old Man and the Sea*, brothers." (Flora 1982, 150). "Big Two-Hearted River" takes place in Michigan's upper peninsula, a part of the state in which, at the time of Hemingway's writing, travel was difficult in the extreme; thus Nick can travel the area for two days without seeing another human and with scarcely any evidence of the existence of others. Despite his isolation, Nick finds community, if only with the trout, the blackened grasshoppers, and himself. Like Huckleberry Finn, who finds his way most readily when in the isolation afforded by the river, Nick traverses not only geography, but allegorical landscape as well. Like Faulkner's Ike, in "The Bear," Nick must confront the mysteries of the wilderness alone. Unlike Ike, Nick is seeking a redemption and not an initiation. "Nick is seeking himself by losing himself" (Flora 1982, 153). In each of the works noted above, isolation is used to accentuate the dividedness of the self. In each work, the protagonist is in reality two characters, boy and man, or novice and initiate.

Nick, for all his solitude, represents a considerable collection of paradoxes. Hemingway goes to great lengths to indicate the rigors of Nick's establishment of camp and his fishing, yet for all the outward discipline, his reason for coming to this place is to deal with inward turmoil. "Already there was something mysterious and homelike," he says of the campsite, collocating the words *mysterious* and *homelike* in a peculiar way. Joseph DeFalco describes Nick as "virtually in a state of suspension between faith and unfaith. Everything around him suggests despair and pathos; yet he never commits himself to this attitude" (1963, 130). Although he is consuming nature, killing insects and fish, Nick also has a reverence for nature, perhaps engendered by the horrors he witnessed in Europe.

The story can be viewed as a sort of chiasmus, beginning with Nick sitting, ending with Nick standing, and centering on the hanging and the priest's admonition to "Be a man, my son." Viewed in such a way, the story is less about resolution and more about tension—the tension between youth and adulthood, innocence and experience, life and death, war and peace, light and shadow, courage and cowardice. Both the wounded and traumatized Nick and the young man about to be hanged exist within and at the mercy of some or all of these tensions. These forces are larger than the characters of fiction, thus all the character can do is attempt to "be a man" and to live deliberately.

Nick undergoes a positive transformation during the course of the story's two parts. In the beginning of the first part, Hemingway emphasizes Nick's passivity. Aside from sitting, his actions in the first scene of the story are almost all those of observation. Nick "looked" four times; he "watched" five times. Twice some form of "see" is employed. Only after he sees the river swirl, the kingfisher fly, and the trout swim does he begin to become an actor in the drama about him and not simply an observer. By the end of the story's second part Nick is very much an actor, and although he does look back to the river in the final paragraph, this action is prefaced by such a parade of actions that the glance backward is only the hollowest of echoes of the paralyzed watching from the bridge.

There is one facet of this story that, while interesting in isolation, is particularly illuminating when considered in connection with some of the other angling fiction, especially *The Sun Also Rises*: the religious elements and, perhaps most important, the parallels with T. S. Eliot. At the beginning of "Big Two-Hearted River," Nick sits on his bundle "almost like some Waste Land fisher king, surveying the wreckage around him" (Flora 1982, 149). In the course of the story, the undeveloped portions of the country act as a remedy to the destruction brought about by people. Nick, sitting at the edge of the railroad, finds the little town of Seney to be almost obliterated by fire. Getting over his initial shock, Nick begins his foot journey, and, after crossing part of the distance between the town and the river, he turns back to see the destruction in the context of the vastness of the Michigan wilderness: "Seney was burned, the country was burned over and changed, but it did not matter. It could not all be burned. He knew that" (180). Nick undertakes this journey, as Eliot put it, seeking to put his lands in order. The quest is a religious one, a fact that Joseph Flora develops in some detail:

> There is no grail image for what he seeks, but his quest is nonetheless religious. The other Nick stories—continually suggestive in their titles and imagery and motifs of the problem of good and evil and the possibility of faith—should help to prepare us for consideration of "Big Two-Hearted River" in terms of religious quest. Even the very act of fishing has established symbolic value for Western civilization, especially the challenge of Jesus to become fishers. The fish is an established icon for Jesus. (1982, 151)

As Nick returns to the river he is seeking not a single goal, such as fish, peace, solitude, recaptured youth, healing, or redemption. He is instead entering into a complex system of representation that he does not fully understand himself. "Hemingway compresses into the form of the story the needs of generations of mankind to achieve a spiritual balance through ritual" (DeFalco 1963, 145), and *spiritual* should be understood in the broadest possible terms in this case. "Nick's journey toward a 'good spot' for fishing along the river parallels the traditional references to myths of rebirth. He must endure the pain of his own burden to get beyond the isolated and local to the area where spiritual resuscitation is possible" (148).

Just as the beginning of the story evokes a memory of *The Waste Land*, published just two years before Hemingway began work on "Big Two-Hearted River," the ending summons up Eliot's memory as well: "As far down the long stretch as he could see, the trout were rising, making circles all down the surface of the water, as though it were starting to rain" (185). This view, as Nick comes to the end of his journey, vindicates the hope with which he set out from Seney. The hope that a trout will rise is the great ineffable wonder at the heart of fly fishing. It is what makes the sport worth practicing; it is what lends a sort of magic to the stories. In this scene of "circles all down the surface of the water," Nick has found a site of plenty. The simile involving rain, while possible to dismiss as a very natural description, can, with little imagination, be taken as another parallel to *The Waste Land* and the centrality of rain in "What the Thunder Said." Other images of *The Waste Land* can be found in items reminiscent of the tarot reading of Madame Sosostris. While the Madame cannot find the Hanged Man, the story includes a hanging between its two sections. The cards include "something he [the merchant] carries on his back," while Hemingway describes at some length the excessive weight of the backpack Nick carries, the paragraph ending with a probable double meaning: "His muscles ached and the day was hot, but Nick felt happy. He felt he had left everything behind, the need for thinking, the need to write, other needs. It was all back of him" (179). Madame Sosostris's "man with three staves" can possibly be found in Nick himself, walking with his rod case in hand. It is very likely that Nick's fly rod would have been a three-piece outfit, and Hemingway mentions the care with which Nick assembles it (although he gives no indication of how many pieces he assembles).

With these parallels in mind, it is not terribly difficult to see "Big Two-Hearted River" as Hemingway's response to Eliot's work or at least as a response to some of the same stimuli as those that moved Eliot to create *The Waste Land*. The most significant connection between "Big Two-Hearted River" and *The Sun Also Rises* can also be found in the legacy of *The Waste Land*. Jake Barnes, who can literally be found—like Eliot's Fisher King, sitting "upon the shore / Fishing, with the arid plain behind me" (lines 125–26)—is, like Nick, wounded and, like Eliot's Fisher King, emascu-

lated. Both Nick and Jake go to the water in hope of some form of redemption. The results they find, however, are quite different.

As the fly fisherman, throughout these pages, has been described as a
divided character, so can the entirety of The Sun Also Rises be described as
a divided novel. In the midst of this novel is the narrator, Jake, who is a
fisherman. Like the Fisher King of Eliot and Jessie Weston, Jake is impotent and conflicted in much more than just his fishing. His sexuality is in
question, and in the final scene of the novel, he both stops sexual action
with Georgette the prostitute and is stopped in his advances to Brett. The
few pages in which Jake and his friend Bill Gorton go trout fishing on the
Irati River near Burguete are central, not only in being located almost exactly at the middle of the narrative, but in presenting Jake, alone with Bill
for five days, in the simplest social setting of the entire novel. Although
Jake Barnes bears considerable resemblance to Nick Adams in "Big Two-
Hearted River," Jake is elsewhere in the text much more difficult to
fathom due to the swirl of characters that surrounds him. In the fishing
portion of the novel, Jake is alone with his friend Bill Gorton, who, not
insignificantly, is not an expatriate.

While the preceding has attempted to demonstrate the dividedness of
the fly fishing section of the novel, Arnold and Cathy Davidson look at the
entire novel, finding it to resist reductive efforts. The Davidsons describe
The Sun Also Rises as a particularly deconstructive and "writerly" novel,
spending a considerable portion of their article justifying the deconstructive approach. When they do finally begin to engage the text itself, their
insight, while lengthy, is significant, claiming that, upon publication, The
Sun Also Rises actually became three different novels, each at odds with
the others, and none that may be definitely described as the genuine Sun
Also Rises. Rather than finding this conflict bothersome, these critics revel
in it and describe the self-contradictions as the most enduring quality of
the novel. It is oversimplification rather than self-contradiction, they
argue, that detracts from the realistic portrayal of life:

> Moreover, tragedy, self-gratification, and self-satire are contradictory only
> if we insist that the self must always be of a piece, must always be free of

contradiction, and that fiction, mimetically, must reduce itself to the same univocal understanding. Such reductionism is the ultimate violation of *mimesis* in that life, as humans live it, is so rarely consistent as such critical formulae suggest. The perfectly sustained ambiguity of the novel's final line—"Isn't it pretty to think so?"—should remind the reader that *anagnorisis*, the realization or enlightenment that Aristotle so valued as the redeeming end of the tragic plot, is perhaps no longer possible—if it ever really was—except as a critical coda, a critical ideal, a critical fiction. Any final meaning of *The Sun Also Rises* hinges, as we have noted, on something as undefined as the vocal inflection of the written word. Depending on how we read Jake's concluding sentence, we can have a sadder and wiser man *or* a man still hoping against hope that, in another time, another place, happiness might yet be possible. But the final sentence is less Jake's sentence—his fate—that [*sic*] the reader's, and the final point is that, returning to the novel's title and the epigraph from Ecclesiastes, the sun *also* rises, the sun *also* sets, and in many of life's lesser and greater moments it's pretty to think, "Isn't it pretty to think so?" saved and condemned by the ambiguities, the merciful incompleteness of the codes that render life both tolerable and terrifying. (1987, 104–5; emphasis the Davidsons')

These ideas suggest an aspect of the previous story. Nick, hiking toward the Big Two-Hearted River, has been described above as returning to this pleasant place from his childhood because of the difficulties he has found in attempting to live in the complex system of representation that overwhelmed him in the trenches of Europe. What he finds is that even though he has returned to a place that he remembers idyllically, the swamp is still downstream. The world is complex and there is no real escape from that complexity. It is, however, possible to live in that complexity and even to derive comfort from it, as Nick views the converging circles of the trout rises to be a signifier not of chaos but of hope. Jake, similarly, finds himself overwhelmed by similar complexity, yet Jake's end, as suggested by the Davidson quotation above, is not nearly as certain as Nick's. Nick is quite clearly on the path to recovery, while Jake is left uttering a terribly cynical line to an equally troubled character.

A comparison has been drawn in the past between Jake and Nick Adams, but the character in *The Sun Also Rises* who might be best com-

pared with Nick is Bill Gorton. Another way of describing this comparison is to call Bill the post–Big Two Hearted River Nick Adams, while Jake
represents what Nick might have become had he not made his pilgrimage
to childhood haunts at the end of *In Our Time*. The most significant and
telling difference between Jake and Bill is in their responses to the fishing
expedition. Like the interloper Neal in *A River Runs through It*, Jake commits the fishing faux pas of using worms rather than flies, yet unlike Neal,
Jake apparently knows about fly fishing. When the pair reach the Irati on
their first day of fishing, Bill announces that he is "going to fish a fly. You
got any McGintys?" Jake meets the request by producing the requested
flies, indicating that he is an initiate to the fly-fishing world and is choos-
ing instead to sit by the dam and dangle worms with a "good-sized sinker."
Because of the heavy weight, he is unaware that he has hooked his first
fish until be begins to reel the bait in. Besides this degradation of his tac-
tile sense due to his choice of method, his location by the dam, in the roar
of the water, degrades his ability to hear. In his morning of fishing, Jake
catches six fish before retiring to the shade to read a romance novel. Bill,
upon his return, produces only four fish, but they are all larger than Jake's.
Jake describes Bill's appearance at this point: "He was wet from the waist
down and I knew he must have been wading the stream" (121).

It is not insignificant that Bill is described in this way. Michael
Reynolds draws our attention to the prevalence of water imagery in the
novel: "Count up the bathing references and see that *The Sun* is one of the
best-washed novels you have read" (1988, 92). At San Sebastian, de-
pressed by the experience at Pamplona, Jake goes for a swim in the harbor.
Reynolds describes the significance of this swim: "Jake dives deep in green,
dark water, but no amount of water can wash away the week in Pamplona.
The sign reminds us of the purification of baptismal water, the holy water
that washes the soul clean of original sin. Jake's need is real and deep, but
ritual cleansing does not work in modern times" (94). The irony of the
novel, read in the context of Hemingway's entire corpus, is that ritual
cleansing does work in modern times, but Jake does not understand how.
Surrounded by all the other water imagery, the key to deciphering the

novel's overall meaning might be found in Bill Gorton's wet clothes. Like many of Hemingway's sentences, Jake's observation that Bill must have been wading can be dismissed as a mere surface detail, yet Hemingway is not given to excessive or meaningless detail. The reader may discern, even if Jake fails to do so, that by fishing with flies, Bill has caught fewer fish, but they are larger, his smallest being about the size of each of Jake's. More significantly, though, Bill, by entering the water and fishing with flies has reintegrated himself with the world, cleansing himself in much the same way that Nick Adams did on Michigan's upper peninsula. One will re-member that everything Nick did in "Big Two-Hearted River" was per-formed with excessive deliberateness and in a ritualistic manner. Like two travelers who have parted years before, Bill and Jake represent two possi-ble outcomes for the same person. The tragedy of Jake's existence is that he comes to the edge of the river, sits, and looks, apparently unable to per-ceive or accept its healing potential. His moonlight swim at San Sebast-ian indicates that Jake is in search of this cleansing, but, no matter how close he comes to it, he fails to take advantage.

According to Hemingway's son Jack, "Papa wrote with the conviction that an artist had to conquer his own devils. This eventually prompted some disagreements with his early friends, Gertrude Stein and Sherwood Anderson. He invariably seemed to prefer the company of those other artists and writers in Paris who shared the reality of hard work" (5). Jake is apparently unable or unwilling to perform this exorcism and is thus con-demned to maintain an impotent and meaningless existence. Like Nick's wound, Jake's emasculation is at once literal and metaphorical. Reynolds reconnects these themes with Eliot:

> Like *The Waste Land, The Sun Also Rises* focuses on failed sexual relation-ships as metaphors for the postwar human condition. Both poem and novel use man's sexual inadequacies as a sign of his moral and spiritual failings. In the poem the land's fertility is not renewed by needed water, and the rituals no longer work. Similar rituals, both Christian and pagan, fail to restore sexual order in Hemingway's bleak view of modern life: nei-ther the religious feast of San Fermin nor the pagan fertility ritual of the bullfights restore order. (1988, 93)

For both Nick and Jake, the quest is to create order from the chaos of modern life. Each of them can be described as "the typical Hemingway protagonist who attempts to salvage from the disparate experiences a meaningful personal existence" (Sojka 1985, 66), evoking one of the final lines of *The Waste Land:* "These fragments I have shored against my ruins." Just as the Fisher King of Eliot's dark vision is attempting to forge some sort of order from the fragments of modern life, so Nick and Jake make a similar, though less allusive, effort. The heroes of all these works behave very much like the Fisher King, like the quester, or like some combination of both in the Grail legends as described by Jessie Weston. They are involved in a quest, but are never altogether certain of exactly the nature, the purpose, or the mechanism of that quest. In the Perceval versions of the Grail legend, Perceval, who is instructed not to ask questions, needs only to inquire about the Grail in order to heal the king and bring the land back to health. In the legends, the health of the land is mysteriously linked to that of the king. In "Big Two-Hearted River," the land goes from burnt to fertile as Nick carries out his journey to the river; in *The Sun Also Rises,* Jake's emasculation is seen not so much as a symbol of the land's infertility but of the lostness of his generation. For both these protagonists, fishing is a sport and diversion, yet it is at the same time something more. Nick seems to recognize and embrace this fact; Jake either fails to realize it or willfully turns from it. To fish is to pursue not only meat but redemption and healing in the Arthurian romances and in the stories of Hemingway. The very title Fisher King derives, according to Weston, from an account of Brons, Joseph of Arimathea's brother-in-law, who "caught a Fish, which, with the Grail, provided a mystic meal of which the unworthy cannot partake; thus the sinners were separated from the righteous" (1993, 116).

Although Jake is often read as the most balanced character in the novel, one should not overstate that conclusion without recalling that Jake provides the narration of both his actions and those of his associates, calling into question his objectivity and credibility. Michael Reynolds claims that Jake is a serious professional: "He may pretend that his job is not important to him, but his sense of who he is depends, in large part, upon his journalism. He saves his earned money to spend his vacation in Spain. He thinks of himself as a professional, one who sustains himself by his work, and he admires professionalism wherever he finds it" (1988, 68). The operative word here, though, is *sustains*. Jake is deeply embedded in a mercantile view of life. His work is what sustains him. It is what allows him to pay the bills that Hemingway constantly has him paying throughout the novel. Reynolds himself notes that "[t]he only operative value in Jake Barnes' world is that of money. As Bill Gorton describes it: 'a simple exchange of values.' If, when reading the novel, you would put a dollar sign in the margin for every mention of money, you would see how central the exchange of values is in Jake's world" (69).

Jake is rendered impotent not only by his war wound but by his inability to move beyond a mercantile or I-it relationship, a failing that Hemingway underscores most simply on the banks of the Irati as Bill Gorton stands before Jake, wet to the waist. Nick, on the other hand, is well on the way to redemption by the end of his story, having immersed himself in both the simple physical acts of fishing and the spiritual and emotional renewal that Hemingway associates with such activities.

Interlude 5

The Hanging

PROBABLY *every angler has a collection of lures that are extra special. I have several such pieces of hardware that remain in my tackle box, although I will never risk them in the water again for fear of losing them to the many hazards that lie below the surface. Open my tackle box and you will see my magic Rapalla minnow, the one that always gets a fish on the first cast. Beside that you'll find the mystical jigging spoon and my battered first dry fly, but the most treasured of the entire menagerie is a fairly fresh-looking yellow crappie jig. A patch of paint is knocked off the jig's head and a few inches of roughened four-pound line still hangs on to him. Most notable about this jig, however, is the absence of a hook. Push aside the marabou that forms his tail and you'll find the brass stump of what was his hook. How he lost that hook is the core of this tale.*

My spinning reel had not seen its final duty when I left the shores of Lake

Doniphan that spring day. Indeed, when my family went camping at Table Rock Lake in May, I left the Orvis rod case leaning in the garage and grabbed my old dependables. Day after day, however, it didn't seem to matter what tackle I had with me, as my children kept me busy enough that I didn't get a chance to fish. Emily insisted that we had to rent a boat and go inner-tubing, thus I didn't have sufficient funds to rent a boat to go fishing. Alyson couldn't face the idea of a vacation near Branson that didn't include a day at Silver Dollar City. We spent most of that day cowering in the shops out of the rain.

By the next to last day of our trip, I was somewhere on the wrong side of surly. I grumpily ate whatever it was that Penny provided for supper, grabbed my tackle box and rod, and stumbled through the fifty yards or so of forest that separated our campsite from the lake.

I remember once standing in St. Peter's Basilica and watching as an ancient nun walked quickly up to the statue of Peter and kissed his foot. She approached the figure so quickly that it seemed she would smash her teeth out, yet it was clear that she moved in this way out of zeal and not carelessness. That, I imagine, is what I looked like in the last hours of daylight on Table Rock Lake. I clambered over the riprap and found a likely-looking spot. Surveying the water's edge, I noticed how quickly the bottom fell away into darkness. In a couple of spots, fallen trees lay like bleached skeletons on the rocks.

Tying the yellow, half-ounce jig onto my line, I wasted little time getting the lure in the water. I cast once. Nothing. I cast again. Nothing. I brought the rod back to toss the jig out again, but this time as I brought my arm forward, I felt resistance.

I looked up to find my line neatly wrapped a couple of times around a slim tree branch. No tangles—no big deal. Holding my rod in my right hand, I reached up with my left to free the jig. It was all I could manage, standing on my toes, to reach the branch. It would be easier, I determined, simply to break the twiglike branch and then untangle my line from a more comfortable level.

The tree, leafless in May, was clearly dead, and the branch bent only very slightly before breaking. I remember hearing it snap. I remember that ever-so-slight bend in the branch springing back to its regular position.

One of the reasons that fishing rods are flexible is to help the angler in setting the hook. Flexibility, it seems, helps a tree to set the hook as well. When the branch sprang back into position, the line pulled between the tree and the broken twig in my hand. The jig jerked hard against my finger and sank into my flesh. For a long moment, I had no idea of what had happened. I was looking for thorns on the tree but found none. By the time my brain parsed the situation, my sentence had been carried out. I stood, right hand holding a fishing rod that I could not lay down without causing excruciating pain and left hand attached by way of a barbed hook and monofilament line to a branch that vibrated at the uppermost reach of my fingertips.

I tried laying the rod down. That was unacceptable.

I tried pulling the line over the branch. That, too, simply led to pain.

Probably, I have repressed the various motions and incantations that I had to undergo in order to get the line out of that tree. To the best of my memory, it involved extracting and opening my knife with my teeth and then cutting the line with no hands. I'm almost sure that I've forgotten something here, though.

With the line out of the tree, I could at least manage to put my arm and my rod down, but the situation was still less than ideal. I still had a half-ounce yellow jig bouncing about on the end of my middle finger. They say that everything is relative, and I would agree. A half ounce, suspended by way of a fishhook from your finger, feels like twenty pounds.

Being the good Boy Scout that I am, I quickly referenced my memory for the proper first aid. Surprisingly, it came back to me almost immediately. I could even envision the unsettling picture that had accompanied the text in my Scout handbook. The solution, the book had suggested, was simple. If the fishhook is embedded past the barb, do not attempt to take it out the way it came. That's why the barb is there in the first place, after all. The proper treatment is to push the point on through a second time and then cut off the barb or the lure or whatever.

"Push it on through?" I shrieked to myself. There was no way I could do that.

I tried soaking my hand in the lake, hoping that the immersion would soften my skin and allow me to pull the barb back out. Returning to camp, I grabbed a handful of ice from the cooler and attempted to deaden my finger in preparation for the trauma to come. That was a vain hope. I almost—almost—allowed my wife to grab the bend of the hook with pliers and pluck the invading body out with a single, horrific jerk. Finally, though, cursing the lost chance to pursue fish that probably weren't even there, I piled my kids and myself into the van and let Penny drive us into Branson to the emergency room.

The doctor, with the help of a local anesthetic, pushed the point on through and clipped the hook off with a rather grimy looking pair of needle-nose pliers.

I'd like to say that this experience has made me swear off anything besides fly fishing, but that would be less than true. I do, however, find that it has given me a certain amount of sympathy for the fish.

6

Big Two-Hearted Writer: Part Two

THE gap between the writer and the narrator is often a difficult one to ne-
gotiate, and in the case of Hemingway this is especially true. Hemingway
himself discussed the difficulties inherent in navigating these straits:

> When you first start writing stories in the first person if the stories are
> made so real that people believe them the people reading them nearly al-
> ways think the stories really happened to you. That is natural because
> while you were making them up you had to make them happen to the per-
> son who was telling them. If you do this successfully enough you make the
> person who is reading them believe that the things happened to him too.
> (1984, 5)

In his two great fly-fishing stories, Hemingway presents two very different fishermen. Nick Adams found in the fishing expedition to the Big Two-Hearted River an opportunity for redemption; Jake Barnes, on the other hand, came to the very banks of a river that seemed, given the imagery of the novel, to offer the same promise of redemption, yet he did not or could not avail himself of that benefit. The question that one might naturally ask in reading these stories is which of these anglers represents Hemingway himself.

The biographical urge is apparently irrepressible in literary studies. Despite the protests of critics old and new, who suggest that the author's background is irrelevant, many, if not all, readers tend to gravitate toward a biographical reading at one level or another. The difficulty that emerges in such readings is the same one expressed by Yeats in "Among School Children": "How can we know the dancer from the dance?" The fiction presented in Hemingway's fishing stories and in many other fishing stories (and perhaps all literature to some degree) is fabrication, yet it is at the same time, as Hemingway notes in many of his comments on writing, a fabrication formed from that which the author knows. In A Moveable Feast, he tells of deciding "that I would write one story about each thing that I knew about" (1964, 12). A 1949 letter to Charles Scribner includes this comment: "A writer, of course, has to make up stories for them to be rounded and not flat like photographs. But he makes them up out of what he knows" (1981, 678).

Hemingway embraces the personal, yet he does not overly privilege it. His advice to F. Scott Fitzgerald is telling in this regard: "Forget your personal tragedy. We are all bitched from the start and you especially have to be hurt like hell before you can write seriously. But when you get the damned hurt use it—don't cheat with it. Be as faithful to it as a scientist— but don't think anything is of any importance because it happens to you or anyone belonging to you" (1981, 408). Good writers, presumably, have learned to use the personal but have at the same time learned not to overestimate its importance.

Despite the possibility of considering the text as an isolated artifact, there is nonetheless something of the author in the story and something of the story in the author. Interestingly, the descendants of Ernest Hemingway have, by their own admissions, been thoroughly buffeted by the urge to make connection with the considerable force that was their famous ancestor. Jack, Hemingway's son by his first wife, recounts a return not to the river of his youth but to that of his father's youth. Jack attempted to retrace his father's steps to the Big Two-Hearted River with a friend in 1941, assuming that "it must have fish in the swampy section my father had described in his short story . . . that we had all read in school." As they drove, the river "looked less trouty by the mile." "The place where we hit the river . . . was disenchanting, to say the least. We were prepared for the tea-colored water, but the pure sand bottom, the marginally warm temperature, and the featureless straight-away from the edge of the sand dunes . . . were not calculated to raise our hopes of catching trout" (1986, 51). They caught nothing and ended up with the car stuck. "Years later I told my father about the trip and he said the Big Two-Hearted never was much of a year-round trout stream after the logging and the fires. He had loved the name but fished another place" (53). In a later story, Lorian Hemingway, granddaughter of Ernest, tells of a compulsion to fish for marlin. If Hemingway's intention in "Big Two-Hearted River" was to suggest that, Thoreau-like, one should accept the forces at work in the world and live deliberately, then it seems that his family missed this message entirely.

Beyond the Hemingway family, other followers of the author have felt compelled to follow literally in his footsteps. H. Lea Lawrence offered *Prowling Papa's Waters*, a travel book in which he ventures to all the fishing spots featured in Hemingway's writing. The first chapter of Lawrence's book offers considerable discussion of the reason why the Big Two-Hearted River was not really patterned after the Two-Hearted River of Michigan, but was instead drawn from the Fox River. Hemingway himself is noted as saying the same in Jack's book, but the more important question than, What river was Nick Adams really fishing? is, Why should we care what river Hemingway had in mind? While a reader who knows Dublin well might find a richer experience in *Ulysses* than one who does not, what reader really needs to know the rivers of Michigan or the Irati in Spain in order to fully appreciate Hemingway's stories that take place on those rivers?

Bryn Hammond describes the compulsion toward the biographical in his study of the culture of trout fishing, *Halcyon Days:*

> Many trout anglers think that Hemingway's "Big Two-Hearted River" is the best fishing story ever written. There is a Two-Hearted River in the Upper Peninsula of Michigan in the same area where Hemingway fished as a young man, but it was a poor trout stream even in those days. Almost ten years later, writing in a Paris apartment above a lumber yard, Hemingway struggled to write a key short story that would somehow knit and hold together (as well as pad out to book size) his first collection of short stories. He already had his alter ego character, Nick Adams, in several of his earlier stories. Now he took Nick trout fishing in the Upper Peninsula.
>
> Hemingway looked back on summer days of boyhood fishing the Fox River with a gang of school friends. But now he had Nick Adams go back there alone, as a man, after a war, and because he liked the sound of the name better he called it the Big Two-Hearted. The scene was true enough, but it incorporated the most memorable features of every river Hemingway could remember. But the fishing was how Hemingway preferred to remember it for the purposes of his story, and in so doing he created yet another Hemingway myth. Even to this day tourists flock to the Big Two-Hearted on pilgrimages along the Hemingway trail. Just as they go to bars in Key West and Bimini where Hemingway never drank, so they go to the Big Two-Hearted River where Hemingway never fished. (1994, 60–61)

The purpose of these examples is not to berate Jack or Lorian Hemingway, H. Lea Lawrence, or anyone else who writes in this vein or who makes pilgrimages to famous fishing sites, but rather to examine the impulse that leads to this sort of writing. At the same time the impulse toward the biographical is considered, another should be taken up as well. Just as difficult to resist as the biographical urge is the interpretive urge, a fact evidenced by the enormous quantity of criticism to be found on Hemingway and scores of other writers. Hemingway validates the evaluative project, indicating that "books should be judged by those who read them—not explained by the writer" (1981, 368). At the same time, he resists many of the interpretations that he feels are forced upon his work, a reaction that is understandable considering the lengths to which many writers have gone in assessing his work. One critic presented a particularly involved reading of *The Old Man and the Sea*:

> It is clear, I think, although Hemingway is working within the Christian tradition, that Santiago (Saint James, the supplanter) wishes to replace its law—the father's—emphasizing meekness, humility, and self-abnegation, with more elemental virtues stressing pride, honor, and killing. The marlin that Santiago kills is both the Other in himself and the law. On one level the marlin is his brother, while on another he is the law of the father that Hemingway would supplant. Hemingway's conscious and unconscious narratives blend in order to give us the complex multiple layers of *The Old Man and the Sea*. . . . The discourse of the Other requires only one metonymic substitution, namely writing for fishing in order once again to elicit all the attributes of a champion. (Stoltzfus 1991, 198–99)

Stoltzfus reaches this conclusion by running through a number of semiotic diagrams showing that a signifier can have two or more signifieds, the skeleton of the fish representing not only his success but death as well (196). Thirty-five years before the publication of Stoltzfus's Lacanian reading, Hemingway, in a letter to Harvey Breit, suggests that each critic is simply the proponent of a theory into which the critic attempts to fit the author's work (1981, 867).

Perhaps in response to the early attempts to dissect his novel, Hemingway, in a letter concerning *The Old Man and Sea* and its critical reception, claims that there is nothing beneath the surface to decode: "Then there is the other secret. There isn't any symbolysm [sic]. The sea is the sea. The old man is an old man. . . . All the symbolism that people say is shit. What goes beyond is what you see beyond when you know" (1981, 780). Four years later, in a letter to Harvey Breit, Hemingway becomes still more specific, attacking a prominent critic. "Carlos Baker really baffles me. Do you suppose he can con himself into thinking I would put a symbol into anything on purpose. It's hard enough just to make a paragraph" (867).

In considering the biographical and interpretive urges that are felt and then expressed by readers, the reader is drawn toward an evaluation of the text and its relationships with external forces. The biographical urge attempts to deduce what of the author has been laid into the lines of the story. The interpretive urge attempts to discover what codes, known by the reader, are present in the story's pages. Seen in this fashion, reading is analogous to fishing. The extensive catalog that Hemingway provides of the tools of the writing trade echoes his detailing of the tools of the angler in "Big Two-Hearted River":

> The blue-backed notebooks, the two pencils and pencil sharpener (a pocket knife was too wasteful), the marble-topped tables, the smell of early morning, sweeping out and mopping, were all you needed. For luck you carried a horse chestnut and a rabbit's foot in your right pocket. The fur had been worn off the rabbit's foot long ago and the bones and the sinew were polished by wear. The claws scratched in the lining of your pocket and you knew your luck was still there. (1964, 91)

Beyond the mere trapping of the angler and the writer, the analogy continues in the processes of each skill. Where the fly angler casts flies, the writer casts sentences, each shaping the offering to match the purpose and situation to which it is delivered. Closely related to the writer, of course, is the reader, whose activity is similarly analogous to the angler's. The reader attempts to "read the river" of the text and make a connection with its creator-inhabitant.

To understand the biographical and interpretive urges, it is necessary to examine further the parallels between writing, reading, and fishing. Writing, reading, and fishing are all pursuits possessed of certain similar qualities. All three appear to be simple, yet are incredibly difficult to master. In a 1935 letter to Ivan Kashkin, Hemingway describes writing as "something that you can never do as well as it can be done. It is a perpetual challenge and it is more difficult than anything else that I have ever done—so I do it." (1981, 419). Writing, like fishing, is not something that one comes to all at once, but is a continuous and never-ending process of learning. "The hardest thing in the world to do is to write straight honest prose on human beings. First you have to know the subject; then you have to know how to write. Both take a lifetime to learn" (1976, 183). Writing in 1951 to Charles Scribner about *The Old Man and the Sea*, Hemingway described his novel as "the prose that I have been working for all my life that should read easily and simply and seem short and yet have all the dimensions of the visible world and the world of a man's spirit. It is as good prose as I can write as of now" (1981, 738). One would assume that the author of *The Sun Also Rises* and *A Farewell to Arms* had reached the summit of his craft, yet he avers here that even after *The Old Man and the Sea* he has still not reached his goal.

One of the qualities that makes writing difficult is that it, like fishing, does not have as its ultimate goal that which it would seem to have. The ultimate goal of the angler is not simply to catch fish, hence the old proverb *Piscator non solum piscatur*. Likewise, the ultimate goal of the writer is not simply to relate a story. Neither, however, is the writer's aim, at least for Hemingway, to encode secret meanings into the text. Instead, the writer, in the process of relating the story, brings to life characters and creates both space and time within which those characters can function. This is similar to what happens for the anglers in Hemingway's fiction. Nick Adams, separating himself from society, creates space within space. He reorders the world in which he lived, a very significant action since the war has left his world seemingly disordered. Santiago, in *The Old Man and the Sea*, exists for three days and nights in a world bounded by the gunwales of his boat and the tenuous connection with the great and largely unseen fish below. When, at the end of *A River Runs through It*, Paul Maclean is described catching a mighty trout, he is portrayed as if in his own world, observed from "high on the bank" and "in the distance" (1976, 97), effectively in his own world.

Like the anglers about whom Hemingway and Maclean write, the writer that Hemingway is attempts, by the practice of his craft, to create and reorder the world. In a 1933 letter to Mrs. Paul Pfeiffer, Hemingway describes his project: "I am trying to make, before I get through, a picture of the whole world—or as much of it as I have seen. Boiling it down always, rather than spreading it out thin" (1981, 397). He expresses a similar sentiment in another letter in which he once again uses a geographical metaphor to describe the ineffable product he is attempting to create: "What I've been doing is trying to do country so you don't remember the words after you read it but actually have the Country. It is hard because to do it you have to see the country all complete all the time you write and not just have a romantic feeling about it" (1981, 123). The reader and writer, like the angler, must see things as they are, placing truth at a premium.

For Hemingway, the reader's proper role as an interpreter was similar to that of an angler. Rather than attempting to impose some external theory upon the river, the angler, especially the fly angler, attempts to live successfully in the world of the river. Similarly, the reader is asked by Hemingway to live within the world created within the fiction and to experience that world's events. He describes this role as follows: "All good books are alike in that they are truer than if they had really happened and after you are finished reading one you will feel that all that happened to you and afterwards it all belongs to you; the good and the bad, the ecstasy, the remorse and sorrow, the people and the places and how the weather was" (1976, 184). A key word in that passage is *truer*. Truth is a central goal for both Hemingway and Maclean.

For Maclean, the value of truth is expressed as he attempts to move closer to the essential qualities of things. This attempt is related to Norman in the story by both his brother and his father. During the book's final fishing trip, Norman asks Paul how he had managed to ascertain what the trout were eating:

> He thought back on what had happened like a reporter. He started to answer, shook his head when he found he was wrong, and then started out again. "All there is to thinking," he said, "is seeing something noticeable which makes you see something you weren't noticing which makes you see something that isn't even visible."
> I said to my brother, "Give me a cigarette and say what you mean."
> (1976, 92)

In this exchange, both brothers strive toward a more complete and accurate view of reality. Paul stifles his initial response and revises it. Norman insists on a specific telling of Paul's general rule. In his discussion with his father, Norman once again experiences the gradual movement toward truth:

"What have you been reading?" I asked. "A book," he said. It was on the ground on the other side of him. So I would not have to bother to look over his knees to see it, he said, "A good book."

Then he told me, "In the part I was reading it says the Word was in the beginning, and that's right. I used to think water was first, but if you listen carefully you will hear that the words are underneath the water." (95)

In the book's final pages, Norman's father interrogates his son over the murder of Paul. In dialogue taking place within the space of a page but explained as occurring on two separate occasions, Rev. Maclean asks Norman no fewer than eight questions regarding Paul's death. In the end, the question that seems to haunt both father and brother is, "Do you think I could have helped him?" (103), for which neither has an answer.

While Maclean allows the reader to extrapolate the primacy of truth as well as his inability to reach it, Hemingway discusses the matter in a straightforward manner: "Good writing is true writing. If a man is making a story up it will be true in proportion to the amount of knowledge of life that he has and how conscientious he is; so that when he makes something up it is as it would truly be" (1976, 215).

Truth in writing is closely related to directness. Hemingway had little use for or tolerance of obscurity.

> If a man writes clearly enough any one can see if he fakes. If he mystifies to avoid a straight statement, which is very different from breaking so-called rules of syntax or grammar to make an effect which can be obtained in no other way, the writer takes a longer time to be known as a fake and other writers who are afflicted by the same necessity will praise him in their own defense. True mysticism should not be confused with incompetence in writing which seeks to mystify where there is no mystery but is really only the necessity to fake to cover lack of knowledge or the inability to state clearly. Mysticism implies a mystery and there are many mysteries; but incompetence is not one of them; nor is overwritten journalism made literature by the injection of a false epic quality. Remember this too: all bad writers are in love with the epic. (1932, 54)

Clarity is valued from the overall argument of the writer's work to the level of syntax and figures of speech. Hemingway is, of course, widely known as a writer of simple and direct sentences. In A Moveable Feast, he describes Ezra Pound as "the man who taught me to distrust adjectives" (1964, 134). In a letter to Bernard Berenson, in 1953, he declares similes to be "like defective ammunition" (1981, 809).

With the ultimate aim of the writer and, presumably, of the reader being truth, the reader's impulses toward biography and interpretation become more easily understood. The task of apprehending the truth that lies at the heart of what Hemingway would describe as good writing is as difficult as Norman Maclean's attempt to come to terms with Paul's death. Maclean ends his narrative without resolving this issue, saying, "I am haunted by waters." The reader, as postmodernist theory would insist, must come away with a less-than-perfect understanding of the text that has been read.

The act of reading "Big Two-Hearted River," and perhaps the act of reading any literature, is similar to the process that Nick undergoes in the course of the story. The reader, with Nick, draws away from society to a secret place in hopes of a healing or an enlightenment. Joseph Flora suggests that Nick is experiencing a sort of Cartesian self-discovery, beginning by stripping away everything that cannot be absolutely trusted and reducing his belief system to his own personal *cogito ergo sum*. Only then, presumably at the end of the story, can he hope to once again move forward (1982, 153).

Flora's interpretation, however, might be criticized as overly simple. Just as successful fishing does not consist of drawing the large fish out of the river, successful reading cannot be circumscribed to the creation or discovery of a closed system of signification. Instead, successful reading involves a continuous exploration of the relationships implied in the biographical and interpretive urges.

> As a secret place, the Big Two-Hearted River says much about such places in the minds of fishermen. They are rarely quite so secret or so desirable as fishing paradises as the myths about them suggest. But mistaken identity can likewise creep into the most seemingly factual accounts of such anglers' eldorados. Let the peripatetic, ever questing fisherman beware: the best fishing is usually around the next bend. (Flora 1982, 61)

At the heart of both fishing and writing, just as at the heart of both reader and writer, there exists a terra incognita of mystery. The desire to map out this territory is what brings writer and reader to the text, just as the desire to master the water is what brings the angler to the river; however, at a deeper level, it is the unknowability of this region that maintains the fascination of these pursuits for their followers. Hemingway, in a 1952 letter to Harvey Breit, expresses the attraction of this mystery: "In truly good writing no matter how many times you read it you do not know how it is done. That is because there is a mystery in all great writing and that mystery does not dissect out. It continues and it is always valid. Each time you re-read you see or learn something new" (1981, 770).

Interlude 6

The House Divided

I TOOK *up fly fishing to give myself a bit more realistic view of my survey of the place of fly-fishing literature in the overall watershed of American letters. What I found upon achieving a certain level of proficiency and knowledge in the sport was that it was without a doubt more pleasant to pursue than the textual creation I was supposed to be forging. As summer dragged on, I found myself obsessing more and more on the actual pursuit of fish with a fly rod and focusing less and less on the writings of Hemingway, Lyons, Maclean, and all those other people whose names escape me right now. It was not only their names that escaped me as June turned into July turned into August. They escaped me; their books escaped me. Most important, probably, was that my computer keyboard escaped me. I was, to steal a nautical term, becalmed.*

I must say that there were a number of compelling reasons why fishing was preferable to dissertation writing at this point. I could buy books or I could buy fishing gear. Borders sat across town from my house, with Barnes and Noble only a little nearer; the Orvis store was just a couple of miles down the road, on the way to the home of my brother-in-law the dangler. Books, by the time you bought everything you really needed, were certainly no cheaper than was the fishing gear. Plus, the books, once read, were largely useless. Oh, I could read them again, but I knew that I probably wouldn't. Besides, the paperbacks, which were all I could afford in most cases, held up most deplorably in the face of midsummer Missouri humidity on the side of a stream.

Don't get the idea that I had given up. Far from it, I must insist. Several times I went fishing. For a day trip, I would toss a Haig-Brown volume in the backseat of the car; for a camping expedition, a couple of anthologies might find their way into the top of my backpack. It never failed, though, that a cooler or my waders box or something would end up thrown in the backseat at the last moment, smothering poor old Haig-Brown for the entire weekend. The backpacked books fared no better. Always, it seemed, a last-minute rain jacket would find its way at the top of the backpack, and, since it never seemed to rain that summer, the books were never heard from again. In fact, one slim volume I gave up for lost, only to find it months later when the dangler talked me into accompanying him on a Boy Scout camping trip.

I know now that I was just stalling. I was avoiding. My mind rationalized a thousand reasons why I should not work on the dissertation today. Fishing was preparing me for the work ahead, right? I was gathering firsthand research. Fishing was a life skill, but for this degree I was just going through the motions, wasn't I? Deep down, of course, I knew the truth. Fishing was not really an obsession; it was an opiate, designed to blunt the pain of not finishing this project.

Late August brought the beginning of school and the reduction of opportunities to fish, but still I managed to squeeze a few hours here and there. I found myself stealing out of the house in the hazy, predawn hours and spending a few precious moments at the local lake. On weekends, I would find an excuse to head south to some Ozark stream or river, often only for a few short hours on Saturday.

Maybe it was the beginning of school and the return to the expectation, vain though it was, that my students would actually make an effort to write something worth reading. I'm really not sure what brought about the change that got me moving once again, but it happened, as August was about to slip into September.

I found myself sitting in my office, with its insufficient shelf space and walls that don't go all the way to the ceiling. I found myself drifting down the Eleven-Point River in canoe. Placing the paddle across the gunwales, my hand found the cork grip of my rod. Back the rod bent, and then, springing forward, it sent line, leader, and fly looping toward a likely-looking spot where a short riffle passed some exposed tree roots. The line rolled onto the water, followed by the leader. With the tiniest of splashes, the fly finished the entire, beautiful cascade by dropping exactly where I had wished. I sat for a moment, the fly's hackles barely dimpling the water and then—SMACK!

It was no fish, but a realization that smacked me on the side of the head. I couldn't just experience this and replay the scene in my head over and over again, the way my kids watch and rewatch The Lion King. I had to tell someone. I had gotten religion and now had to become an evangelist or I'd never get this fishy smell off my hands.

My hands flew to the keyboard before me. Without much thought, I began to lay out my experiences one after another. The sights, the smells, the sounds—all of it came rushing back to me there in my cramped little office. I typed, a stupid-looking smile plastered across my face as I trotted out my equivalent of a "What I Did on My Summer Vacation" essay. After a furious little spate of writing, I pushed back from the desk and admired my craft.

"Dave!" I called down the hall.

"Yes?" my friend answered. I heard his chair squeak. He knew my "come here" tone of voice well enough.

"Check this out," I said when he appeared in my doorway. I had never asked him—or any of my colleagues for that matter—to read any of my nonacademic work, and Dave was the furthest thing from a fishing enthusiast I could imagine. His idea of an outdoor adventure is grilling burgers on his deck.

He leaned over the back of my chair and read. After a moment, I found myself reading it aloud as he followed along. And he did follow. He listened and enjoyed.

That was when I realized that I had contracted the malady that I was studying. Like the myriad fly-fishing writers whose books line the shelves at Borders and the thousands more whose yarns are spun over coffee or dinner, I had felt compelled not just to experience the river and its wonders but to bring that wonder back to the rest of the world—or at least to Dave.

When I got home that afternoon, I scarcely said hello to my wife. Instead, I went straight to my computer and set to work on the next chapter of the dissertation. After my office experience, it seemed like the most natural thing in the world to do.

7

A Visit to *The River Why*

COREY Ford, one of the better outdoor writers from the 1930s until his death in 1969, introduces a collection of his stories with a question:

> Why do people fish? Nary a word is to be found amid all the encyclopedias and books in the world to explain what perverse impulse, what freakish strain, what incomprehensible urge causes an otherwise normal and sane citizen to don a pair of uncomfortable rubber waders, lace a dozen pounds of hobnailed boots onto his aching feet, truss himself helplessly in canvas vest and landing net and creel, and hike upstream ten miles in a pouring rain, fighting midges and black flies, scratching his face on brambles, wincing whenever the elastic strap of his landing net catches on a twig and lets go like a slingshot, smacking him smartly between the shoulder blades. (1995, 15)

The question arises often. In David James Duncan's novel *The River Why*, the narrator, Gus Orviston, whose father is a world-renowned fly fisherman and whose mother is an accomplished bait angler, seeks out the meaning in life by devoting himself completely to fishing. At the same time that Gus maintains his single-minded dedication to fishing, his younger brother, Bill Bob, seeks to find enlightenment by attempting to engage simultaneously as many of the nonfishing activities of the world as possible, going so far as to listen to two radios tuned to different stations —one in each ear. The question that each brother attempts to answer, each in his own way, is the age-old question: Why?

In a particularly angst-filled moment of the novel, Gus accompanies his brother to the top of a nearby peak and the pair look onto the valley below. Bill Bob, who has never shown any interest in "any stream, puddle or glass of water before," notes with admiration the shape of the river that stretches before them, causing Gus considerable curiosity: "I asked him why. He laughed and said that that was exactly what the river was asking me. I'd no idea what he was talking about" (79). Only considerably later does Gus arrive at the import of his brother's words: "There were the letters, there was the word: plain as water, in a flowing, utterly uncrabbed hand, current, erosion, gravity and chance had written 'why' upon the valley floor! Billions of ever-changing, ever-the-same gallons of gurgling sun-and-moon-washed ink, spelling forever, in plain English, 'why.' It was incredible. It had to be kidding. Rivers can't write, let alone ask questions"(131).

Although, at this point in the novel, Gus has reached an important realization in his quest to balance his life, he still has a good many miles of water to cover. Having seen that the river itself is asking him the question, however, he is able to begin to formulate an answer.

Similarly, at some boundary point in humanity's past, when evolution and technological advancement had made angling an avocation rather than a necessity, anglers much like Gus, felt the compulsion to ask why one fishes. This question must have arisen soon after the absolute need to fish had turned the practice into a sport, yet it persists to the present. As has been seen in the survey of the angling literature of the previous several centuries, this question of why humans fish has been a persistent one, drawing responses from virtually all important fishing writers. By the end of the twentieth century in North America, the fly fisher, perhaps more than any other, must ask this troubling question. Faced with dwindling and overpressured waters to fish, the fly fisher might easily retreat to the much more available and accommodating waters of the many reservoirs that dot the map, yet fly fishing enjoys more practitioners now than ever. And the river continues to ask "why?"

Undoubtedly, the most obvious potential answer to the question of why humans fish is that we do it in order to catch and eat fish. As has been discussed above, such an obvious answer has been accepted as self-evident in the majority of British angling writing produced over the past two centuries. On this side of the Atlantic, the father of North American dry-fly fishing, Theodore Gordon, sounds very similar to his British progenitors, describing his best day of fishing completely in terms of the twenty pounds of fish it produced (1990, 89).

While Gordon's attitude seems focused almost completely on the catch as the purpose of the fishing, later American anglers have taken a more complicated view. One writer notes "the happiest American invention of all, ever to influence the world of fly fishing. This was the fishing book in which few, if any, trout were reported slain, and where the decorations were generally in the form of drawings of living fish, rather than dreary photographs of very dead corpses of once proud trout" (Hammond 1994, 11). If one is to believe much of recent angling literature, for the late-twentieth-century fly fisher, fishing is more than just catching fish. In fact, some would have us believe that catching fish is simply not that important.

Paul Quinnett, however, does not accept that sentiment, nor does he trust those who espouse it, claiming that regardless of what people say, "you and I know that people go fishing to catch fish." Quinnett claims that a person who does not care whether fish are caught cannot truly be a fisherman. "You don't have to keep them, eat them, photograph or frame them, but you do have to catch them, at least once in a while" (1994, 44).

After the catching-fish response to the question of why many take up fly fishing, another potentially important answer can be found in the words of Theodore Roosevelt, who, although he was discussing big-game hunting, might easily have been dealing with fly fishing, a sport that he also practiced. Roosevelt described two attractions of hunting, the chance to be in the wilderness and the opportunity to exercise "manliness and hardihood" (204–5). As regards the first of these attractions, many fly-fishing writers have commented on the habit of trout to live in beautiful places. One does not find populations of rainbows in the dredged and channeled shipping rivers of the world. Ted Leeson is one of many to comment on this happy coincidence of nature, describing as a "wonderful mystery" the very existence of fish. He concludes that the presence of a beautiful fish in a beautiful body of water is something so extraordinary as to provide an absolute bearing for the angler's moral compass (1994, 117).

Christopher Camuto states a similar sentiment in a much simpler manner, suggesting that "[f]ly-fishing requires good taste in rivers because trout have good taste in rivers" (1988, 50). It is, according to these writers, however, not enough simply to visit a beautiful place and observe a beautiful species. According to Bliss Perry, "the man with a rod or gun sees more and feels more in the woods than if he were to go empty-handed" (1927, 52).

Roosevelt equates the quality of a hunt with its difficulty, noting that the pursuit of some mountain species "demands more hardihood, power of endurance, and moral and physical soundness than any other kind of sport, and so must come first" (1990, 208). The same test that Roosevelt applies to the hunting of game is applied by many to the pursuit of fish. Like John Kennedy, speaking of the quest to place humans on the moon, fly fishers choose to do these things not because they are easy but because they are difficult. Continuing this parade of presidents, Herbert Hoover outlines the hierarchies of methods that fishermen employ, running from dry flies, through wet flies, spinning tackle, to bait. He respects this stratification, but does acknowledge that "toward the end of the day when there are no strikes, each social level collapses in turn down the scale until it gets some fish for supper" (33–34).

That these and other American politicians can be found expressing the same attitudes toward hunting, fishing, or the ultimate outdoor pursuit, space exploration, is not coincidental. The desire to accomplish that which is difficult or nearly impossible, whether it be catching a huge trout on a gossamer tippet, "taming" the vastness of the American West, or safely placing astronauts on a lifeless rock a quarter-million miles away seems to hold a place of honor in the pantheon of American virtues. Perhaps just as significantly, the success of the venture is not as essential as its difficulty. Far more has been written about the "one that got away" from a fly fisherman than of all the carp or catfish ever caught in America; more is made of the "failed" Apollo 13 mission than of all the successful lunar landings. Another way of synthesizing Roosevelt's two primary reasons for outdoor pursuits would be to look at them as drawing humans into the best that nature has to offer, while at the same time drawing out from the hunter or angler the best that that person has to offer. In essence, then, outdoor sport, in its best form, would bring together an entire array of superlatives.

Excellence, in its many incarnations, can be found to be a dominant theme not only in the work of Roosevelt, but also that of many others before and after him. In one of his gloomier moods, Nick Lyons decries the urban and academic worlds in which he is forced to gain his livelihood, yearning instead for the challenges and beauties that the trout stream offers:

Only suddenly, bursting in on me, would be some city image, like that cab driver pounding the Cadillac with his hammer or one of those prissy colleagues of mine at the university who laughed only at literary jokes, told me my fish writing would destroy my academic career, and could not say four words without uttering a *mise-en-scène* or a *raison d'être*. We were hooked up to so many wires: we were wired to our past and to the drug of the media and to the itch—oh, it was always there—to get on and make it and prove who we were and play not in our own game with our own rules but in the world's game. (1977, 110)

While Lyons finds himself focused on the overall ambiance of his sport, Bliss Perry is especially drawn to the excellence represented by a more restricted object, his tackle: "A three-or four-ounce split-bamboo rod, with a well-balanced reel, a tapered casting-line, a leader of the proper fineness, and a well-tied fly or flies, is one of the most perfectly designed and executed triumphs of human artisanship. A violin is but little better" (1927, 35). Perry continues his discussion in a manner that might suggest Icarus in its emphasis on the artifice of the sport:

> The very artificiality of the means employed heightens the enjoyment of fly-fishing. You choose deliberately the lightest tackle that will hold the fish. Perhaps you use a barbless hook, to increase the odds against you. At any rate, you give the fish a sporting chance. You neither net nor spear nor dynamite him. You challenge him to a trial of wits, his against yours. (36)

Perry, one can see, does not follow a single line even in restricting himself to a discussion of tackle, but rather combines and overlays issues such as the technical excellence of the rod, the willful choice of the most difficult method, and the challenge inherent in the sport. For him, and for others who will follow, the answer to the great "why" question is not a simple one. Following Archilochus of Paros, he describes foxes as those who know many things, but hedgehogs as those who know the one big thing (1927, 26).

> Fishing in general has always seemed to me a form of subversion anyway. In a world that insists upon "means" and "ends," that dooms every path to a destination, fishing elides the categories and so slips the distinction altogether. You become engaged in the nonterminal, participial indefiniteness of "going fishing." . . . To go fishing is essentially functionless, though that's not at all the same thing as saying it is without purpose. (28)

One writer goes so far as to describe winter fly fishing as subversive (Leeson 1994, 28).

Angling writers seem nearly as easily drawn to the spiritual realm as they do to discussions of paradoxical elements of their sport. In explaining the attraction that fly fishing holds for its practitioners, many writers attempt to bridge the gap between the sacred and secular, either opting, Walton-like, to see angling as a means toward the divine, or, in a more contemporary manner, to frame the sport as a means toward self-discovery and awareness. In his study of trout-fishing culture, *Halcyon Days*, Bryn

Hammond notes the propensity for angling writers to reach for the divine: "Despite our addiction to fly fishing, those of us so addicted deep down long for the universal approval we heap upon ourselves as God given. Angling literature is full of such divine posturing. None so better or succinct, to my mind, than a melodious passage from Norman Maclean's *A River Runs through It*" (1994, 87). Maclean himself, of course, drew Hammond's (and many others') attention with the following lines:

> In our family, there was no clear line between religion and fly fishing. We lived at the junction of great trout rivers in western Montana, and our father was a Presbyterian minister and a fly fisherman who tied his own flies and taught others. He told us about Christ's disciples being fishermen, and we were left to assume, as my brother and I did, that all first-class fishermen on the Sea of Galilee were fly fishermen and that John, the favorite, was a dry-fly fisherman. (1976, 1)

Where Hammond seems to look somewhat askance at "divine posturing" and Maclean's protagonist appears divided in his description of the family's beliefs, another writer can be found who quite unabashedly embraces the spiritual aspect of fishing. For Herbert Hoover, "next to prayer, fishing is the most personal relationship of man" (1963, 76), and "[f]ishing is a chance to wash one's soul with pure air, with the rush of the brook, or with the shimmer of the sun on the blue water" (11). Far from an impractical dreamer, Hoover suggests that fishing offers a solution to crime problems: "Lots of people committed crime during the year who would not have done so if they had been fishing. The increase of crime is among those deprived of the regenerations that impregnate the mind and character of fishermen" (21). While Hoover elsewhere writes of descending to less challenging methods in order to avoid coming home empty-handed at day's end, he also proclaims his belief in the old maxim, *Piscator non solum piscatur:* "Fishing is not so much getting fish as it is a state of mind and a lure for the human soul into refreshment" (30).

Where some of the foregoing writers seem to be relating a fairly tepid brand of twentieth-century Protestantism, Ted Leeson reaches back over the millennia for a spiritual aspect of fishing. He quotes Aristotle's *Physics* as saying that the governing principle of nature is that everything seeks its origins. People cannot fly because the body is composed of soil and thus held to earth. The spirit of man, on the other hand, is of heavenly origin and thus tends upward. Leeson, a writer who tends steadily toward the metaphysical, asserts that this fact is the only one that gives him a reason to discuss dry-fly fishing in metaphysical terms (155–56). For Leeson, the dry fly, floating half in, half out of the water, represents the divided nature of humanity.

While a few writers such as the preceding follow Izaak Walton's lead in drawing religious significance out of the rivers they fish and the trout they catch, a much larger group can be found engaged in a spiritual quest of a more secular nature. For this relatively large group of anglers, the reason— or at least one reason—for fishing is not to find fish but to find oneself. Like Zen meditation, fly fishing becomes a route to self-awareness in the writings of many of the most celebrated angling writers of recent years.

Nick Lyons, probably the most influential fly-fishing writer working today, proclaims that after a day on the river, "Our thoughts will be greener, our judgments perhaps sharper, our eyes a bit brighter. We live day to day with little change in our perceptions, but I never go to a river that I do not see newly and freshly, that I do not learn, that I do not find a story" (1977, 22). Continuing to celebrate the transformative qualities of rivers, Lyons compares the waters of his memory with two bodies of water that figure enormously in both American nature writing and the American personal essay.

> They are my Pilgrim Creek and Walden Pond, however briefly. Those
> rivers and their bounty—bright and wild—touch me and through me
> touch every person whom I meet. They are a metaphor for life. In their
> movement, in their varied glides, runs, and pools, in the secrets we seek to
> understand about ourselves, our purposes. . . . When such rivers die, as so
> many have, so too dies an irretrievable part of the soul of each of the
> thousands of anglers who in their waters find deep, enduring life. (23)

While the river, for Lyons, is an external agent of personal change, he at the same time identifies the river with the self. The familiar river, as demonstrated from the following pair of quotations, is not just a comforting relic from the angler's past, but is, because of the manner in which angler and stream insinuate themselves each into the life of the other, actually a part of the angler. Lyons first notes that "something in us hungers for the familiar, the known, the pleasure of fishing water that we know like the freckles on our arms" (1989, 50), but then, while describing how his old home pool on the east branch of the Croton had changed dramatically when a huge tree washed away, he adds that a "part of us gets washed away at such times, too" (52).

The current study has previously suggested that one manner in which one may view literature, or virtually any creative act, is as an ongoing attempt to answer the question of what it means to be a human. Following this line, one might assert that fly fishing is an attempt by the anglers not simply to catch fish but to catch themselves. This is certainly a key point of departure between the fly fisher and most other anglers, although to label intentions wholly based on the angler's methods would be simplistic.

The best answers to the question of why people fish seem to follow similar lines of thought. There is no simple answer that is completely satisfactory; therefore, the most thoughtful writers who attempt to arrive at an answer succeed most notably, like Lyons, in complicating the question. Ted Leeson, whose *Habit of Rivers* is an extraordinary look at the philosophical aspects of fishing, complicates the question by emphasizing that the relationships forged in the act of fly fishing are not confined to a meeting between the angler and the fish:

> To some temperaments, fishing appeals most deeply as an approach to a web of relations that give shape and coherence to the natural world. Fly fishing in particular embraces the kind of minutiae that weave themselves into ever enlarging contexts. A trout stream points backward to geology and atmospherics, to history and evolution; it leads forward to insects and fish, to hydrology and botany, to literature and philosophy. Connections branch and rebranch in overlapping associations until finally, from the pattern of venation in a mayfly wing, you can reconstruct an entire watershed. In this regard, fly fishing is entirely self-explanatory, for by nature it revolves around on its own most revealing image—the riseform. The rise

of trout to a drifting insect reverberates in expanding, concentric ripples, magnified iterations of a simple event that resonate outward to encompass more and more, remaining visible long after and far from the thing that made them. The rings of a rising trout eventually comprehend the entire river, yet no matter how large their compass, like all circles they never cease to invite an inference of the center. (1994, 3)

However, the urge toward complication is not, at least on the surface, absolute, as the following passage from Paul Quinnett demonstrates:

If you sort through all the things fishing includes—daydreaming, rod-building, fly-tying, camping, scenery, solitude, friendship, the love of nature, tradition, relaxation, a balm for the soul, and so on—what you find at the very core of angling is the thrill of getting hold of a wild thing, a creature that will, reliably and predictably, spend its entire essence in a struggle to break free from bondage. (1994, 45)

While Quinnett's attitude might appear more reductive than Leeson's, one way of reading Quinnett's words does not require such a narrow approach. Quinnett is not altogether clear as to what exactly he refers to in speaking of "a wild thing, a creature that will, reliably and predictably, spend its entire essence in a struggle to break free from bondage." Presumably this creature is the trout or the salmon that the fly fisher pursues, yet that assumption begs the question of what exactly the angler is pursuing. The angler might be simply pursuing the fish, yet there are other, equally valid answers to that part of the question. Like the hero of Hawthorne's "Great Stone Face," the angler might set off in pursuit of the fish, yet find that the really valuable quarry is at the thicker end of the fly rod. The "wild thing" that Quinnett pursues might be truth or understanding or even the answer to the question of why people fish.

Jack Curtis, in the introduction to a selection of his stories, expresses a sentiment that can be profitably viewed alongside Quinnett's:

The act of fishing can be the act of catching an idea with all the energy and sophistication we can cast into the deepest mind pool. To catch the fish is to catch the insight, whether fry or whale, an epiphany as Joyce applied it to literature. The fish is a bright thought, an illumination, brought from the depths after a ritualistic preparation within nature. (1988, 47)

In an autobiographical story, "Grandfather," Curtis gently develops his broader answer to the question of why one fishes, detailing the way in which his grandfather used fishing to get him interested in reading and academic success.

> Reading became interesting, writing turned into a mirror game, a challenge much like trophy fishing. Writers kill themselves driving against their impossible ideal standards, the same as fishermen extend their strength and resources to catch the impossible fish. There at the round oak table in grandfather's kitchen was the origin of a dozen novels, anthologies of short stories, volumes of poems, many, many fishing stories. All from a kid who had practically ceased to function in the educational process. God love my grandfather. (69)

The question of why humans fish leads to the question of why humans who fish feel compelled to write about it, which leads to the question of why some humans feel compelled to write at all. This last is another question that has seen a multitude of attempts toward an answer but no wholly satisfactory answer. Just as many who write can offer no clear reason for a compulsion that, in the vast majority of cases, makes no sense according to the traditional priorities of society, most who fish would struggle to offer a coherent explanation as to why they stand hip-deep in fifty-degree water on the first day of trout season.

Ultimately, it seems, the best answer to the question why humans feel compelled to fish is that they fish in order to ask the question. Fishing is, by its nature, an uncertain and interrogatory endeavor. By engaging in this endeavor—or in writing, composing, painting, or any of a hundred other pursuits—the angler moves out of the realm of the known and into a creative realm of questions.

Of all the singularities that are used in order to explain what makes humans the dominant and unique creations that we are, perhaps none is more powerful than the human urge toward creativity, an urge that invariably begins with a question. Bryn Hammond traces this trait back to our earliest ancestors:

No doubt, that first one of our primitive ancestors who forsook the net or trap or spear and took to the river bank or sea coast to fish with a rudimentary rod and line, and fished as much for pleasure as for food was looked upon by his fellows as being peculiar and out of step with the world of reality. And perhaps in those sentiments we reach as close as we are likely to get into the heart of the matter as to why men fish. Maybe that first and apocryphal sports fisherman was, albeit unconsciously, stepping outside the real world as perceived at that time. If that is so, as I suggest it may be, then we anglers who fish today are similarly, if fragmentarily, turning our backs on what most of our fellow humans call the real world. (1994, 1)

Hammond may oversimplify. For the angler, the act of fishing is a step away from the real world at the same time that it is a step into the real world. The difficulty involved in answering the question of why humans fish is perhaps a testament to the difficulty of precisely plotting the line that separates those two worlds. The persistence of the question stands as a tribute to the evolving examples of our species who live determined to inhabit both worlds.

Interlude 7

The End of the Rainbow

THE day that Dave read the first of these asides over my shoulder came after all the events that these little tales describe. With that word of warning out of the way, I'd like to back up a few months to my first big fly-fishing expedition. Yes, I had made the trip to Lake Doniphan, but after fighting the wind and the obnoxious little kid, that one hardly seemed to count. This time, I was serious. Finals were over, grades were submitted, and I was heading south.

Having left home early, I found myself on the side of Lake Taneycomo at ten o'clock. The water, as can be expected, was there; the fish were presumably there. The problem was that I didn't have a very clear idea of what I was supposed to do. Taneycomo, I should probably explain, is nothing like the other Ozark lakes that paint the map like sprawling, blue Chinese dragons. Taneycomo follows the course of the White River, beginning at the foot of the hulking concrete wall of Table Rock Dam and ending at a relatively modest dam, some thirty miles downstream, at the upstream end of Bull Shoals Lake. When power is being generated from Table Rock, the current in Lake Taneycomo is ferocious. At other times, it's simply a gently flowing hundred yards or so of water.

After walking around as much of the lake as I could manage without feeling like I was just avoiding putting a fly on the water—which I suppose I was—I picked a spot that required walking nearly a half mile from my truck and then half-climbing, half-sliding down a thirty-foot embankment before reaching the water. I chose the spot partly because it was away from the hatchery outlets upstream, where I felt the fishing would be less than sporting, but in reality, my main reason for picking this spot was that I knew there would be few if any others fishing nearby to see my fumbling attempts.

I wasted little time getting my rod assembled and tying on a size-twelve scud—the fly that the Orvis lady had suggested to me. Surveying the spread of water before me for a likely target, I gently rocked the rod backward and listened to the whistle of my scud zipping through the air. All was well as the rod flexed forward and sent my fly out toward the stump I had selected. I hadn't released nearly enough line, by choice, so, after several false casts, I stripped out another four feet and lengthened the cadence of my casts. I was still on target but about eight feet short of the stump. Stripping off more line, I arched the rod back once again, but this time, as the spring of the graphite urged itself forward, I felt a tug, much like that I'd felt just a couple of miles away on the shores of Table Rock when I'd impaled myself with that little yellow jig.

I turned around to find my fly clinging to a willow branch, looking every bit as if it were hanging on for its life, afraid of being offered to the ravenous Taneycomo rainbows. With a snort of disgust, I carefully—and I must emphasize, carefully—removed the fly from the branch and waded out a bit deeper, hoping to create backcast room for myself by moving off from shore.

It was about an hour that I spent in that spot, carefully picking my spots as I waded farther out and made many—probably over a hundred—casts. At one point, I set my left foot on the submerged roots of a tree only to have the sodden dirt between two roots give way and allow me to plunge neck deep into the water, filling my waders with fifty-degree water. On the other hand, I also spied a shadow beneath a huge, drowned sycamore trunk. It looked to be a fish, so I set my sights on placing my fly right on top of that shadow. After a couple of frustrated attempts, I let go a cast that rolled, perfectly, and dropped the fly with scarcely a splash right into the middle of the shadow. The shadow, of course, didn't move, much less strike at my fly, but that didn't matter. The cast had been perfect, and, for a moment, I understood the beauty of this sport.

I didn't understand it well enough to spend much more time on this wretched stretch of water, however. Plodding onto the shore in my waders, wet inside and out, I struggled up the embankment and made my way to my truck. After a lunch at the Taco Bell in Branson, I drove back to the lake for a little more frustration.

This time, rather than torturing myself with a remote and difficult stretch of water, I headed straight for one of the hatchery outlets. There, I was joined by a couple of guys who looked as if they had just stolen away from the welding shop for the afternoon.

"Feels like we're in A River Runs through It, doesn't it?" the thinner, more energetic of the pair said, apparently to me. The second guy didn't break out a rod and scarcely spoke, but his companion brought out a fly rod, surprising me.

"You had any luck?" he asked as soon as he had a line in the water.

"No," I answered. "But I just got here." I didn't feel compelled to tell him about the morning and filling my waders. Here, I was safe and dry and warm on a rocky bank. There was no need to dredge up the distant past.

"Yeah, they're pretty tough to get at with all the rain we've been getting," he added.

A couple of hours oozed by on that spot. We could see foot-long trout scooting around in the clear depths of the inlet, but they showed only the slightest interest in our offerings. About an hour into our afternoon, my companion made a discovery.

"Hey, Chris," he beckoned to his friend. "Looky there!" Following the line of his arm, both Chris and I squinted and craned our necks attempting to see what he was seeing. It took a moment for the images to sort themselves out, but when they did, it was clear what had piqued his interest. A huge rainbow, nearly two feet long, lay at the bottom of the deepest part of this little inlet. I couldn't imagine that something that big had passed in front of us without our noticing, so the only conclusion was that he had been sitting there the whole time.

"Look, his mouth's kinda messed up," Chris pointed out.

Sure enough, we could plainly see some whitish scar tissue at the top of the trout's mouth. Although aesthetically troubling, the monster's appearance did nothing to dampen our enthusiasm. We wanted him.

For another hour, we both dragged flies, floated flies, hung flies, and everything else that we could think of in front of this beast, who lay there on the bottom like a piece of waterlogged driftwood. With the afternoon burning away, I decided to call it a day and head back for my camp. After breaking down my rod, I bid the pair goodbye and headed back for the truck. I had just thrown all my gear in the back seat when I heard a scuffle of voices from the shore.

"Hey, Chris! I got him! I got him!"

"Easy, don't lose him!"

"Get the net! I got him!"

"Okay, I got it. Easy. Run him over here."

They then bayed like coonhounds. I started to walk back over and see the sight, but decided to let them have the moment for themselves.

8

How I Fished and What I Fished For

ONE of the great American fishing writers of the first part of the twentieth century, Alfred W. Miller, wrote under the name Sparse Grey Hackle. "With a roar like a werewolf, Sparse could not hide that he was really mostly a gentleman and a lamb. He practiced a code from another, nearly forgotten time, and it included strong doses of honor, steadfastness, loyalty, dignity, backbone, pride, the art of making truly careful sentences and the art of being a gentleman, and love" (Lyons 1989, 215). As a former reporter for the *Wall Street Journal*, Hackle is said to have "imputed to the world of fly fishing, which he loved deeply, a sense of character and tradition and wit; he saw it as a human activity, full of wonder and excitement, far beyond the mere catching of fish—an activity that enlivened the heart and sparked the imagination. It had the power to bring out the best in men—and some of the worst" (215–16).

This profile of a man renowned as both angler and writer points out a commonality between the fly-fishing traditions of the Old and New Worlds. Fly fishing, whether done by petty nobles in Britain or by merchants in upstate New York, was—and is—a pastime of persons of character. One was expected to behave in a certain manner and to fish in a certain way.

Methodology is, to fly fishing and, consequently, to its literature, a central concern. For the professional bass angler, bait is forbidden by the rules; without such rules it would doubtless be employed. For the purist fly angler, bait is unconscionable. The appeal of fly fishing is in its difficulty and in its beauty.

Beyond the question of why people fish, there is the question of how they fish, a subject that for the fly fisher involves a whole series of choices, beginning with the fly itself, working its way up the tippet, the line, down the rod, to the reel, and ultimately into the very person of the angler. Perhaps in no other sport is the old adage more true: "It's not whether you win or lose; it's how you play the game."

One of the ways in which Americans play the game of fishing creates such a spectacle as to warrant television news coverage each year. The opening day of trout season in many locales finds hundreds—perhaps thousands—of anglers lined up, shoulder-to-shoulder, casting for their limit in the hatchery-supported waters of a state park or river. The trout parks, and similar sites around the country, are not accepted as suitable locales for quality fishing by the elite of angling writers, and, while these elite writers are guilty of their share of snobbery, such does not seem to be the source of their aversion. Robert Traver, presumably writing about those who pursue their trout in less-traveled waters, describes the attitude as opening day draws near. "The true fisherman approaches the first day of fishing with all the sense of wonder and awe of a child approaching Christmas" (1989, 3).

Anglers who take advantage of stocked, hatchery trout are not the only examples of those who do not represent the ideal of fly fishing as expressed by its literary tradition. In detailing the proper method, several writers have seen fit to give readers at least a quick glimpse at the wrong way to fish. While fishing is often glowingly described as an act of coming into a state of concert with nature, Ted Leeson observes that just like the construction of dams and luxury homes, fishing can potentially devolve into an act of domination over nature. Rivers, he points out, provide humans with various opportunities for unflattering self-expression (1994, 116).

Another aspect of fishing as an act of domination is found in the professional bass-fishing events as described by Nick Lyons: "Fishing by the clock, for pound and number, against other superstars of the Hawg-Bass circuit is, on any scale of values, a desecration of the sport. Fishing is not a competitive sport, at least not as I understand it, nor are its rewards so easily tangible" (1989, 187). In Jim Harrison's celebrated essay "A Sporting Life," greed is defined as a force antithetical to the proper enjoyment of outdoor sport.

> Outdoor sport has proven fatally susceptible to vulgarization based mostly on our acquisitiveness. Fishing becomes the mechanics of acquiring fish, bird hunting a process of "bagging a limit." Most sportsmen have become mad Germans with closets full of arcane death equipment. To some, an ultimate sport would be chasing coyote with a 650cc snowmobile armed with an M-16. . . . Hunger causes the purest form of acquisitiveness, but our tradition always overstepped hunger into the fields of hoarding and unmitigated slaughter. The saddest book printed in our time is Peter Matthiessen's *American Wildlife*, where the diminishing and disappearance of many species are minutely traced to our greed and game hoggery. Sporting magazines still publish those obscene photos of piles of trout, though there does seem to be a change in the air. (164)

Howell Raines describes his earliest fishing memory in which he "learned the emotion of rank greed" (1994, 41) in catching an apparently endless string of crappie from a bridge in Alabama. Raines's memoir, *Fly Fishing through the Midlife Crisis*, details the process by which he moved from the acquisitive type of fishing—what he terms "the Redneck way"—to a more satisfying and wholesome method.

Harold Blaisdell, a contrarian in most things, resists the value judgments that most fly-fishing purists would attach to the various types of angling:

Most of us shape our creed to conform to whatever level we may reach in our evolution as fishermen. The more discriminating our preferences, and the more convergent our interests, the more closely our piety approaches fanaticism. This is well and good, for it is only when viewed from such a position that the act of taking a twelve-inch trout on a dry fly becomes a feat of marked significance. (1969, 365)

Notwithstanding Blaisdell's dissenting view, it will be noted that most fly-fishing purists place not only certain methods but also certain species in a position of privilege over all others. Among the changes that came to Howell Raines during the years he chronicles is the realization that some fish are more worthy to pursue than others. William Humphrey points out that

[t]he trout is not, "pound for pound, and ounce for ounce," as game as the black bass, but who is the black bass's Theodore Gordon, the hermit saint of trout fishing? The catfish provides sport for a greater number of people, yet the best-selling book on fishing of all time, after *The Compleat Angler*, is entitled *Trout*, and rightly so; if you do not agree, whether you be a fisherman or not, try *Catfish*. (1978, 17)

Taking an opposing view to these species elitists, however, is Blaisdell, who suggests that species chauvinism such as Humphrey's is out of keeping with proper fishing: "Quite possibly this is the key to fishing: the ability to see glamour in whatever species one may fish for. Regarded objectively, a fish becomes a prize worth seeking only when we endow it with romantic qualities which are the products of emotion" (1969, 11).

Despite this one dissenting view, conventional wisdom seems to stand heavily in favor of a certain hierarchy of species. Even when only trout are considered, it is widely agreed that some are more sporting than others. A central and apparently valid complaint often leveled by fly-fishing purists against hatchery-raised trout is that the fish are simply not as worthy a prey as those that are born and learn to survive in the wild. One writer presents the opinions offered when a "group of casually surveyed ichthy-ologists . . . abandoned their normally cautious and nonanthropomorphic language to describe hatchery fish as 'dumb,' 'foolish,' 'stupid,' and 'very stupid.' The fly-fisherman is not flattered when one of these 'man-made' fish takes his handmade lure" (Hope 1984, 167).

The careful angler has little interest in a careless fish. While the hatchery trout is widely viewed as a careless feeder, the same cannot be said for its stream-bred relative, as the following account of the fish's feeding habits will attest:

> [T]he wild trout is a model of efficiency in its feeding. It spends 86 percent of its day facing upstream, in a precise and sheltered stream-bottom location where the push of the current is minimal and where it can carefully survey the multitude of food and nonfood items drifting downstream. When the fish catches sight of an approaching insect, it rises, inspects it close up, sucks it in, and immediately slides back to the bottom, repositioning itself in exactly the same sheltered location as before. (ibid.)

Just as the trout is a creature of habit, so the angler is a creature of tradition. To some, this tradition is merely a set of images with which to associate oneself (Tirana 1996, 14), but, at a more significant level, tradition is a value to the fly fisher for more than simple aesthetic reasons. Certainly the image cut by Brad Pitt in Robert Redford's screen adaptation of *A River Runs through It* is striking, yet just as fly fishing prowess does not suffice for Paul Maclean, neither does appearance suffice for the modern angler. In the introduction by Alfred W. Miller (Sparse Grey Hackle) to George La Branche's influential 1914 book *The Dry Fly and Fast Water*, one finds the following testament to tradition: "In a changing world, angling is one of the least changing of the arts. Over the years, the fish have not changed nor have the insects. Save in detail, the tackle has not changed, either" (vii).

La Branche, however, is not chauvinistically attached to tradition. His book, dealing almost exclusively with methodology, was written to deal with the changing challenge brought to American trout fishing by the introduction of European brown trout to American waters. Despite bringing innovative techniques to American anglers, La Branche balances the forces of change with a voice of conservatism. The joy of the catch, he suggests, "should be measured by the method of capture" (150).

The importance of method in the world of fly fishing and its attendant literature can scarcely be overemphasized. Methodology not only brings together tradition and innovation, but also provides a definition for fly fishing. It only stands to reason that if fly fishing is, in the minds of its most devoted practitioners, superior to other methods, and if dry-fly fishing is superior to wet-fly fishing, then there might be any number of further distinctions to be drawn regarding method, beginning with the obvious, the equipment, and proceeding to the less obvious, internal elements.

> Fly fishermen often use delicate equipment; they can discuss fly patterns and leader tapers ad infinitum; the peculiar flanged tail of someone's Hendrickson spinner is critical; they study entomology and brood about the morphology of rivers. Fly fishermen probably read more [than other anglers], and with a more discerning eye. They must be aestheticians as well as hunters. The fly-fisher's sport demands more of him—and he knows this. He is generally less interested in how many fish he catches than in how they were caught. Because of all this, the philistine's cry of "Snob!" may well be met with more than a trifling sense of superiority. (Lyons 1989, 185)

Difficulty is a virtue for the purist angler and for most angling writers. Since dry-fly fishing is (arguably) the most difficult method to employ, it maintains a position of privilege among most anglers. Jack Hope describes the manner in which a singular difficulty of fly fishing, the fly itself, leads to several others:

> The flyfisherman, because of his choice of a tiny lure that commonly weighs less than .01 ounce, must use an elaborate and perfectly timed series of motions to achieve a cast of even 30 feet, especially in wind. This forces him to wade close to his skittish prey and , if he hooks a one-pound trout, to work it to the net with infinite patience and delicacy to prevent his gossamerlike leader from breaking. (1984, 163)

William Humphrey delves into the subject of methodology and finds a similar conclusion when he notes that the "reason that all other kinds of fishermen look up to the dry-fly purist is not that he catches more fish than they; on the contrary, it is because he catches fewer. His is the sport in its purest, most impractical, least material form" (1978, 38). Humphrey goes on to argue that the dry-fly fisherman does not envy the others their better catches, and, while they "regard him as daft and subject him to much joking, down deep those other varieties of fishermen have a sneaking admiration for his quixotry, and yield him without grudge his place at the top of the ladder" (39).

After the trout itself, the focus of fly fishing must be on the fly. In the sequence of objects that leads from the mouth of the fish to the hand of the angler, the fly is the first over which the angler has significant control. As noted above, the fly is at the same time the source of many of the difficulties implicit in fly fishing and the factor that makes the sport possible. Graig Spolek, writing in the *American Journal of Physics*, describes the fly as follows:

> Fishing flies are designed to imitate floating insects. They are very light with a relatively large volume of feathers and fur so the surface tension acting on the large surface area can "float" the fly. Because of the large surface area, the fly's motion during a cast is easily dominated by air friction. For example, to cast a typical fishing fly horizontally 20 m from a height of 1.5 m, and no line were even attached to it [sic], an initial velocity in excess of 140 m/s (313 mph) would be required, a prohibitive condition indeed. The solution to the flyfisher's dilemma is to cast a rather massive line to which the fly is attached and allow the fly to go along for the ride. As a result of this symbiotic relationship between line and fly, the fly (as the launched object) demonstrates a behavior during flight that is unique from all others [lures]: it accelerates horizontally. While this effect may be intuitively disconcerting, the predicting physics are quite straightforward. (832)

Even in his attempt to describe the flight and attendant physics of the fly, Spolek seems unable to avoid descending into mildly philosophical verbiage, discussing a symbiotic relationship between fly and line. Those whose audience and purpose do not urge them toward scientific detachment move even further in this direction.

Many writers agree that the fly is central and primary to the art of fly fishing. Its size determines the rod, the line, the reel, and all the equipment of the modern angler. Ted Leeson suggests that, beginning with the fly, one can infer not just the late-twentieth-century fly fisher who casts that fly but all the attendant equipment of that angler and, in fact, the complete history of fly fishing that lies behind (1994, 48).

In Leeson's scheme, the fly is not only primary in its position at the end of the fly line and at the center of the sport's history, but occupies an important position at, and as the end of, the sport.

> It forms the terminus of all our preparations, study, practice, and observation. . . . The angler's part of fly fishing begins and ends with the fly, and everything in between—the tackle, the planning, the preparations, the trip, the reading and wading of water, the casting—all are ancillary, mere vehicles for delivering the fly from vise to trout, for transferring it from one set of jaws to another. (48)

So central is the fly to the sport that a huge proportion of the jargon and peculiar terms derive from fly patterns. Central figures in the development of the sport have immortalized themselves by attaching their names to new fly patterns, most notably Theodore Gordon, who developed the Quill Gordon and many of its variants. Moving the other direction, Alfred W. Miller, adopted the name of a fly, Sparse Grey Hackle, as his pen name.

Although the centrality of the fly cannot be argued, there is a considerable emphasis placed on another piece of equipment, the fly rod. Sparse Grey Hackle, writing for a 1942 edition of *The Anglers' Club Bulletin*, presents a remarkably laudatory profile of Hiram Lewis Leonard, the designer and builder of the hexagonal, split-cane fly rod. What is noteworthy about this piece of journalism is not that Leonard should be the subject of an article in a fishing periodical but the manner in which he is presented, a manner evoking memories of nineteenth-century biographies of Washington and Lincoln.

For the avid fly fisher, however, Leonard can be seen as little other than a legend, a craftsman who, by carefully splitting and recombining cane in a particular manner, transformed what had been a relatively stiff and unresponsive tool into something approaching the modern fly rod. While modern materials, notably fiberglass and more recently graphite, have supplanted cane as the medium of choice for quality fly rods, there remains a devoted core of anglers who find the natural, split-cane rod preferable on both an aesthetic and a functional level.

Whether made of cane or of graphite, however, the fly rod transcends simple utilitarianism. Like hunting firearms, fly rods (and to a somewhat lesser degree other fishing rods) hold a place as works of art or at least excellent craft. One maker of fine fly rods, William Reading, describes his work as the transformation of a cold material, graphite, into a work of art (Franson 1993, 28). The magic of the rod, despite its aesthetic appeal, lies mainly in that which it can accomplish for the angler. The fly, central to the sport, remains a static and useless bundle of feathers and fiber without the splendidly tapered grace of the fly rod to put it in motion. Fly casting is, while not as difficult as some would suggest, surely a complex and challenging physical act. A computer model of a typical cast required about six hours of processing time on an IBM PC with a math coprocessor using IBM Professional FORTRAN (Robson 239), yet again the scientific description does not do justice to the action.

Fly casting seems to demand metaphor. For Norman Maclean, that metaphor was derived from the clock and its rhythms. According to the narrator's father in *A River Runs through It*, fly casting "is an art that is performed on a four-count rhythm between ten and two o'clock." Maclean proceeds to suggest that for his father fly casting was an attempt to gain a connection with the divine rhythms of nature: "As for my father, I never knew whether he believed God was a mathematician but he certainly believed God could count and that only by picking up God's rhythms were we able to regain power and beauty" (1976, 2).

In a significant choice of metaphors for the current study, Christopher Camuto likens fly casting to the human thought process and, more important, to writing:

> The traverse of a mind along its rivers leads on and on. The grammar of fly fishing prose flows naturally toward the promising, hypnotic parataxis a young, unspoiled Ernest Hemingway brought into the mainstream of American literature from the trout streams of a midwestern boyhood.

That style, which Nick Adams borrowed from Huck Finn, who got it from the big river at the heart of the country, is nostalgic and hopeful and poised against man's tendency to destroy. In all its variants, the style, like the backward-seeming effort of casting a fly line, is an attempt to reach into the natural world and confirm its sustaining presence in the lives of men. (1990, 234)

Camuto suggests that the fly cast is an "attempt to reach into the natural world." One of the defining aspects of fly-fishing literature is its awareness and foregrounding of the natural world. As Byron criticized the angler for having no interest outside of catching fish when all about him is the wonder of nature in one of its most beautiful locales, so might a modern Byron criticize certain anglers of today whose focus seems very narrowly attached to the size and number of fish caught. On another part of the waters, however, one finds the fly fisherman, whose attention, while certainly captured by the idea of catching many and large trout (or other species), is equally enthralled by the many and changing natural sights that surround the place in which he fishes. Bliss Perry sees that "the fun and glory of fishing consist in fishing, and not in being 'high rod'" (1927, 33). Russell Chatham, in "Angler's Afternoon," an article from a 1978 *Field and Stream*, details an early-season fishing trip to Yellowstone, pursuing grayling. The story, far from focusing only on the actual fishing, includes a long walk both ways to the river, a downpour, and a stumble on the marshy bank (72). Thomas McGuane observes the apparently natural urge toward a determination of the bottom line in fishing as in other human pursuits. "At the end of a fishing trip you are inclined to summarize in your head. A tally is needed for the quick description you will be asked for: so many fish at such and such weights and the method employed. Inevitably, what actually happened is indescribable" (1988a, 20)

The preference for viewing the world in a broader and deeper fashion is the one that is expressed, completely separate from fishing, in Barry Lopez's essay "The Stone Horse," included in *Crossing Open Ground*. Lopez tells of visiting a remote and ancient horse effigy made of stones in the Mojave desert. He describes the remarkable moment of making out the horse's image but also of several hours of observation, moving about to see the artwork from different angles, and noting the changes to the image wrought by the slowly moving sun. At last, he remarks about such artifacts and their purpose, asserting that they were to be viewed over a long period by those on the ground. "It is our own impatience that leads us to think otherwise" (1989, 14).

This impatience is what sends many people thousands of miles to "do" the Grand Canyon, Yosemite, or Yellowstone, but leaves them so empty of benefit as they depart. Robert Stowell, in the introduction to his collection of maps that Thoreau owned and consulted, indicates that Thoreau understood this human (or European) tendency toward travel as domination. Stowell suggests that Thoreau believed that "traveling, like surveying and map-reading, demanded a serious attitude, a proper spirit" (1970, x).

Among the ranks of fishing writers, we can find several writers who relate strongly to these sentiments expressed by Lopez and Thoreau. For Bliss Perry, "The paradox is that this very preoccupation with angling seems to make him [the angler] more sensitive to the enfolding beauty of the landscape. He must, of course, to perceive it fully, have a certain capacity for philosophical detachment, a kind of Oriental superiority to failure or success" (1927, 54–55). Lopez seems to be traveling the same stream when he notes that with "the loss of self-consciousness, the landscape opens" (1989, 44).

The angler for whom the landscape has opened is not simply a nature lover, but has become a part of nature. For such an angler, the highest and most treasured skill is not the catching of fish but the reading of the river, a sentiment echoed in the words of many prominent fly-fishing writers. Phillip Johnson presents the centrality of reading the river in terms that suggest the ability to read literature: "As any philosopher of angling knows, mastery of the sport lies not in fooling fish, but in reading the river, a profound art that is worth a lifetime's patient study" (1986, 30). Johnson continues to describe the value of the "literature of rivers" as follows: "There are all sorts of sound, pragmatic reasons for learning the language of streams. Still, the deepest motivation may be the pleasure of simply observing and understanding the ebb and flow of a river and its chain of life. Shifting from matching the hatch to reading the river is like graduating from comic books to poetry" (35).

In such a view, fishing becomes much more a process than a product. Just as one can never claim absolute mastery of *Paradise Lost,* one can never claim absolute mastery of even the most local and often-fished river, yet the well-known river, like the well-known poem, takes on a place of profound importance. Familiar rivers, for Ted Leeson, are not just comfortable fishing haunts but places of certainty and true orientation for the angler (1994, 116–17). For entomologist Rick Hafele, the same idea is presented in less poetic terms: "Catching fish is great, but it's not an end in itself. The most important thing is to know the stream" (qtd. in Johnson 1986, 34).

Reading the stream, like reading literature, involves more than simply decoding the literal signs that nature presents. Ted Leeson argues that seeing that which is difficult to see often requires the viewer not to focus directly on the object but somewhat to the side of it, thus allowing it to come into clearest view (1994, 110).

River reading is creative reading, requiring that the reader look at things in a new way while a more easily seen and more familiar old way battles for the reader's attention. In such a scheme, the most intransigent piece of the semiotic equation is likely to be the reader's own predispositions and not any particularly difficult and impenetrable codes that either river or poet presents; the most essential thing to master is the self.

The pinnacle of fly-fishing methodology as presented in the works of many of its most celebrated writers is found in the paradox of what the angler is actually pursuing. Far from the simple pursuit of fish, the best angler pursues self-awareness. This pursuit accepts and even celebrates the notion that good fishing may often be singularly uninfected with caught fish.

One work exploring this notion, William Humphrey's novella *My Moby Dick,* begins by echoing Melville, with the words, "Call me Bill" (1978, 11), yet Humphrey's obsession is far less destructive than that of Ahab. He describes his fishing as "an act as private as prayer" (13). In the story, he stumbles onto a pool containing a three-foot trout: "I wanted that fish and I wished I had never laid eyes on him. I had not lost a leg to him, but he had certainly taken a big bite of my brain" (47).

Throughout the trout season, Humphrey learned to fish with both skill and humility as he attempted to catch that huge fish. On closing day, having graduated to an eighteen-foot, spider-web-thin leader, he placed four successive casts in front of the giant without arousing his suspicion. "Those repeatedly ignored casts made my young companion smirk; I, though rather ruefully, admired my unproductive accomplishment" (92). On the fifth cast, the fish exploded out of the water, taking the fly in mid-air. "At once weighty and weightless, he rose to twice his own length" (93). After three huge leaps, the fish gave a shake and broke the fragile leader. (94)

Humphrey lost the fish, but in retrospect did not mourn the loss. "Would I really rather have that fish, or a plaster replica of him, hanging on my wall than to see him as I do in my memory, flaunting his might and his majesty against that rainbow of his own making?" (95). In the end, Humphrey recognizes that the quality of the fishing was far more important than the number or size of fish that were caught: "Fishing stories always end with the fish getting away. Not this one. This, reader, has been the story of a fisherman who got away. For old One-eye made a changed man out of me" (96).

Humphrey presents, in a most straightforward narrative, the essential qualities of how one is supposed to fish according to the mainstream of American angling writers. Ted Leeson, perhaps the most contemplative of this lot, expresses this essence as follows:

> The craft of angling is the catching of fish. But the art of angling is a receptiveness to these connections, the art of letting one thing lead to another until, if only locally and momentarily, you realize some small completeness. By no coincidence, this is the art of writing essays, as it is, I think, the art of living, for among these three occupations there seems to me no essential difference in degree or kind. (3)

Fly fishing, properly performed, in the view of Humphrey, Leeson, and others, is not a matter of obtaining a thing, the fish, but of creating a particularly rich moment of time and space. This moment might manifest itself differently for different writers, who would typify it variously as peace, enlightenment, or joy, and define it primarily in terms of time, space, or mental state.

Among the writers who best express this creation of a space is Leeson, who describes the phenomenon as follows:

> In the end, to fish well is to cultivate an arrangement of time and place, of circumstance and perspective. We arrange ourselves into the arrangement, and if the collusion is careful and lucky, we reap a kind of enclosed moment of some sharply felt beauty and significance. The particularities of river and landscape, of the trout and the season, of the fisherman and the fishing, all merge, crystallizing the instant into a whole that exceeds the sum of its parts. (177)

Leeson also emphasizes the idea of a created—or perhaps more accurately, re-created—space when he describes the solipsized world created by the angling moment, suggesting that the visible limits of a riverside meadow serve to turn the anglers consciousness inward, forging a world at once bounded and unbounded (149).

For John Gierach, the emphasis on created space is manifested in his book *Where the Trout Are All as Long as Your Leg*, which centers on the idea of secret fishing places. "The secret places are the soul of fishing" (1991, 3), Gierach begins. In an ensuing paragraph he quickly acknowledges and then discredits the emphasis on things and acquisitiveness as the heart of fishing. In the book Gierach spends eighty-nine pages describing a handful of secret places he has known in his years of fishing. Although his discussion seems to be a straightforward treatment of an aspect of fishing of which everyone is aware, there is always the possible subtext of a "secret place" in the spiritual or mental sense. This subtext is never made overt, but its potential existence seems to lurk behind his words. Gierach hints at this "something more" in one of the early tales of the book as he relates a childhood clandestine expedition to a fishing hole considerably outside his normal range. He learned something significant about fishing from this first venture beyond his childhood boundaries:

"that when done properly it [fishing] is socially unacceptable, and that the farther out there you go the better it gets" (17).

While for some the most important dimension of the magical fishing moment is space, for others time figures more importantly. Even in something as simple as a profile of one of the sport's great forebears, one can find the importance of time. One writer describes the father of American dry-fly fishing as follows: "Theodore Gordon was a perfectionist, and he had the time, the skills, the profound curiosity to devote, season upon season to the development of his wood-duck-winged creation" (Leonard 1978, 49). For Gordon, as well as Hackle and many others, fly fishing was not something that could be learned quickly. It required an immense investment in time.

While consuming time, however, fly fishing is also described as paradoxically creating or enhancing time. Nick Lyons is one writer who seems particularly in tune with this aspect of fly fishing. "The clock is crucial. In fact, all trout fishing has been for me a disciplining of my inner clock. In my early years it ran haywire: I rushed and fidgeted and allowed everything and anyone I was with to control the tempo with which I fished" (1989, 197–98).

Lyons describes his temporal discoveries in broad terms above, but grows more specific in a 1992 publication, *Spring Creek*. This book tells of a month spent fishing Spring Creek, "the most interesting river I had ever fished or could imagine." The creek was "loaded with secrets that would take exceptional skill [and presumably time] to learn" (4). In the midst of this fishing, time, for Lyons, seems to change from a linear phenomenon to a sort of montage of varied but related images. A series of passages illustrates this metamorphosis.

> Within a week, the days blurred and I had to concentrate to separate them, keep them in sequence, though I have had no trouble finding in my brain the full and vivid picture of a hundred moments. . . . The clock began to lose significance by the second week and by the fourth was virtually gone. We were on the water when we thought the flies would start and we stayed until we were hungry or blown off by heavy winds and rain. . . . When we fished the Back Channel, the time was merely however long it took to fish

around that bend properly. . . . I became more concerned with *thingness* than *whenness*. I found less and less imperative to create and live within a category of time. (4–5; 137–38; emphasis mine)

Just as important as the metaphor used to define this created moment is the perceived nature of that moment. In almost all cases the moment is described in a positive manner—hardly a surprise, given the predispositions of the writers in question. The moment might be best described as one of freedom:

On any stream, if the fishing goes well, there comes a moment when you reach a plateau of satisfaction. You sit on a bank to rest, lean your back against a tree and feel liberated from the many concerns of your daily life. For a brief time, you get a chance to simply exist, on a par with the birds and weeds and grasses, and it's this moment, more than any other, that you take home with you, along with the uneaten carrots and potatoes, and the leaders still in their packages. (Barich 1990, 18)

For Ted Leeson, the moment created by proper fishing is of a much more spiritual nature. He suggests that, like those involved in the manias of religious, romantic, or poetic pursuits, much of the pleasure derives from the possibility of not ultimately reaching the object of one's quest. For such seekers, the greatest joy comes from the hope for an uncertain reward (1994, 47). Later in his work *The Habit of Rivers*, a book whose title as well as content might be seen to suggest a spiritual life, Leeson describes fly fishing as an activity ruled by faith, an activity that possesses, like all faith-driven pursuits, a controlling miracle, in this case, the trout rising to take a dry fly (155). William Humphrey, in "The Spawning Run," likewise brings faith into the foreground of fishing:

Fishing demands faith. Faith like St. Peter's when the Lord bade him cast his hook into the water and catch a fish for money to pay tribute to Caesar. To catch a fish you have got to have faith that the water you are fishing in has got fish in it, and that you are going to catch one of them. You still may not catch anything; but you certainly won't if you don't fish your best, and you won't do this without faith to inspire you to do it. (1990, 283)

Underlying these professions of faith and hope is the idea of uncertainty. Uncertainty is a value highly treasured by these writers, for in uncertainty there is the potential for surprise. Leeson, in a less religiously oriented moment, expresses this preference succinctly, asserting that predictability is the thing most antithetical to the psyche of the fly fisher. The value of a trout stream, he argues, is at least partially to be found in its surprises (1994, 148). Surprise is valued in either its pleasant or disappointing varieties, for both define the potential for creation. The few ecstatic moments of success in fishing are bracketed by scores of fruitless casts, short strikes, and other failures, yet without those failures, the ecstasy would be much diminished. Leeson points out that American history is full of failed utopias. Fly fishing offers a path to successful utopias, however limited in their scope.

> There are, I think, only moments of local perfection, fashioned from design and chance. . . . A harvest of these brief entireties appears to me a plausible response, perhaps the only one. A life lived recollecting or creating or anticipating such moments, enjoying and appreciating their value, may not possess the seamless continuity that we expect of something like "truth," but it does have the feel of some truthlike substance. And I'll settle for that. (178)

Interlude 8

Crane Creek

AS I drove back to my campsite after a second unsuccessful morning of fishing Lake Taneycomo, I could practically feel the discouragement dripping down my back. Two days and not so much as a nibble had done a lot to dampen the enthusiasm that I had come here carrying. I must admit that I was probably looking for an excuse to give up and head home, but the weather report made that moot. With severe thunderstorms forecast to come sweeping across northwestern Arkansas and southern Missouri later that night, I eyed the little green tent I had swiped from the Scout troop with a good deal of suspicion. No adventurous bone in my body made me desire to ride out a screaming early-summer thunderstorm in a mildewed, two-man tent (which probably leaked anyway). Depositing my camping and fishing gear in the back of the Blazer, I pulled out of the campsite and pointed myself to the north.

I must say here that I've always been smitten by the alternate route. When I first read "The Road Not Taken," I probably found it rather obvious. With a few extra hours to burn and no pressing need to reach home by any certain time, I decided not to take the direct route to Springfield and then to Kansas City, but instead found myself looping along backroads, generally following the path of the old Missouri Pacific Railroad's White River Division. My road wound its way through little knotted Ozark towns such as Reed Springs and crossed the James River on a magnificent, arching bridge at Galena. It was at Crane that I realized I wasn't headed immediately home. Somewhere, from the back of my mind, a glimmer of text found its way to the fore as I pulled away from the town of Crane's lone stoplight. There was a fishing area nearby—Crane Creek. It was strictly catch-and-release, as I recalled, but that was perfectly fine for me.

A mile or so past town, I saw a brown sign on the left of the road indicating that the Crane Creek Fishing Access was to be found two and a half miles down a side road. Hesitating only for a moment, I turned the wheel and heard the crunch of gravel under my tires. A quarter mile down a long hill, I felt as if I'd entered a new world. The barbed wire and telephone poles that had punctuated the highway were gone. A curtain of reddish-brown dust hung in the air behind me as if to close off my last connection to the real world. After twisting down a long stretch of gravel, I found myself as the lone vehicle in a small parking area, fifty feet from the waters of Crane Creek.

Crane Creek, at least the mile or so that I fished, rarely stretches more than fifteen feet from bank to bank. Its water is so clear that you feel tempted to drink straight from the stream, and the pea gravel that lines most of the stream bed builds the sense of perfection. That was it. Crane Creek was perfect.

After walking a half mile or so upstream, I stepped into the rain-swelled current, having abandoned my waders and opted for jeans and duck shoes. The surge of spring-cold water swelled against my thighs. The pangs of the cold shocked me, stealing my breath for a moment, but only a moment. Once my legs adjusted to the cold, I surveyed the stream, up and down its course, until it disappeared around the corners and behind the oaks that arced gently across its width.

I stripped off a few yards of line and began prospecting for a spot to drop my fly. Locating a riffle that made its way past a log, I stripped more line and tossed a cast in that direction. The fly overshot the target, landing in the weeds on the bank. After untangling the hook, I found a new spot and repeated the process. It took a few minutes for me to adjust to the flow of the water and the filtered light of the stream, but before too long I was landing flies very close to where I wanted. Playing with the current, I'd see the fly strike the water just upstream from where I thought a trout might be hanging and watch as it slid past the target spot.

Nothing was happening. For all I knew, there were no fish in Crane Creek. Maybe the guidebook's article was simply a cruel joke, designed to give the locals something to laugh at. I cast and cast, generally putting my fly into what I guessed to be likely water, but with jarring regularity nothing was happening.

And yet everything was happening. Water swirled over rocks and gravel, around bends, and through trees that somehow managed to cling to the banks of the creek. Blue jays cackled from the branches overhead, now and then flitting across the open nave of the chapel of oak that grew around my head. Squirrels barked from the larger limbs of the trees, and damselflies hovered like helicopters over the pulsing surface of the water, periodically touching ever so slightly on the surface. At the same time, my rod was swinging back and forth in a lazy rhythm, flinging the ever-changing loops and curves of line over the water, dropping the lightest of artificial flies ever so slightly on the surface. Everything was happening even though I wasn't getting anywhere close to a trout.

I have no idea how far down the stream I had wandered, but it was far enough that all thought of driving, of eating, or of catching had flown from my mind. It was as if I were no longer aware that I was fishing, but rather that this state of being was my norm. What else should I be doing besides walking in the middle of an icy stream and casting flies?

And then there was a jerk. I wasn't drawing in line at the moment or pulling on my rod. The current was headed the other way. This was no snag, I quickly determined. I was not deluding myself into believing that something vaguely fish-like was happening at the other end of my line. This was a strike.

Of course the time that it took you to read the last paragraph is approximately the same as the time that it took me to think it. By the time I reacted to the fish it was somewhere in the next county. Frankly, I wasn't even sure how to react to the fish. Had I been bass fishing, my response would have been quick and certain. I would have jerked back so hard that the hook not only set but yanked the fish out of the water and into the boat. But despite my considerable reading on the subject of fly fishing, I hadn't the slightest idea whether such a move would be wise.

It didn't matter, though. There were fish in Crane Creek. I was not merely a mad man waving a nine-foot wand of graphite in the air. Crane Creek was perfect. The day was perfect. The fish were superfluous.

9

Ichthys und Du

THE essential difference between the Old and New World forks of an-
gling-writing tradition might be reduced to the distinction that Martin
Buber draws between the I-It and the I-Thou relationships.

> To man the world is twofold, in accordance with his twofold attitude. The
> attitude of man is twofold in accordance with the twofold nature of the
> primary words which he speaks. The primary words are not isolated words,
> but combined words. The one primary word is the combination *I-Thou*.
> The other primary word is the combination *I-It*; wherein, without a
> change in the primary word, one of the words *He* and *She* can replace *It*.
> Hence the *I* of man is also twofold. For the *I* of the primary word *I-Thou* is
> a different *I* from that of the primary word *I-It*. (3; italics in original)

Buber continues his study by saying that these primary words do not denote things as much as they do relationships. The I-It relationship is one in which the human objectifies the it: be it animal, human, or inanimate. The I-Thou relationship, regardless of what the thou represents, is a relationship of mutuality and connection.

Fishing, of course, can be described in terms of Buber's worldview. Those who focus on the catch as the ultimate goal and who see the fish or the river as something to be mastered would be described in I-It terms; however, the mainstream of American fly-fishing writers subscribe to a completely different perception: I-Thou. Fly fishing, for these practitioners, is a method for creating connections of various sorts.

In the universe of fly fishing, the focus would seem to the untutored eye to rest with either the fish or the angler. It actually resides at a point where their two worlds meet, in the molecules-thick meniscus of the stream. The dry fly, resting on the surface of the water, represents a junction point between the aquatic and terrestrial worlds, between the clearly seen world of the angler and the obscured world of the trout. Ted Leeson extends this sense of a point of connection to include a point between the mentally seen and unseen, which suggests and begins to explore the human capacity for imagination and inquiry (1994, 157).

Just as surface tension buoys up the fly on its hackles, so the tension between these two worlds creates the essential appeal of the sport. "What one seems to be is refuted by that which lies just below the surface, and outward manifestations of character represent little more than an uneasy truce between opposing forces of nearly equal strength" (Blaisdell 1969, 356). Leeson expresses this same notion: "Dry-fly fishing emerges on the far side of 'what happens' and fixes itself on the idea of 'where,' on the focal plane of the surface. Here, the symmetrical domains of air and water converge to form both a mirror and a barrier. And I think that the fascination of the dry fly arises from this paradoxical character of the surface, at once richly hinting at the life below, while obscuring our apprehension of it" (1994, 156).

A magical moment occurs when those two worlds come together where the fly lands. This observation would seem obvious to anyone with the slightest understanding of what fishing is all about, yet Leeson describes the instant in a way that uncovers a richness of subtext that is not obvious—perhaps not even to the angler. When the fish takes the fly, the barrier between the two worlds is broken, revealing to both worlds things that were hidden. This moment visually represents the answering of a question or the fulfillment of a curiosity, allowing the angler to realize, if only for a brief moment in a finite space, that understanding is a possibility (157).

Just as fly fishing provides a locus for the merging of the worlds of air and water, so, in a larger sense, does it provide a vehicle for the forging of a great number of relationships or connections. In the previous chapter, the ability of fly fishing to provide a connection between the angler and deeper insight of various types was presented. Other, more tangible connections are also discussed in a variety of writers. These relationships include those between the angler and self, the angler and society at large, and, in the case of the growing quantity of fishing writing by women, between the angler and her gender identity. Leaving human concerns, there are writers who focus on the angler's relation with nature and, ultimately, with language.

The first area for exploration is the angler's relationship with self, which, to a large extent, involves and overlaps the relationship with society as a whole. In *Bright Rivers*, Nick Lyons finds a great deal to describe not only in the bright rivers of the title but in the gray city that he leaves behind in order to go fishing. One implicit irony, which Lyons never actually states in so many words, is that in the midst of so many people, he is unable to make an interpersonal connection. He tells the story of the neighbor in the next apartment with whom he never speaks and who, when diagnosed with a terminal illness, shuts himself off from all human companionship, forcing the police to break his door down. There are all the various persons on the fringes of respectability—the prostitutes, pimps, lunatics, and beggars—but, Lyons notes, "I know no more than ten people among the thousands who live within two blocks of my apartment" (1977, 10). The only connection he seems capable of making within the city is during a meeting when his thoughts turn to rivers. It is interesting to note the ambiguity of pronoun references in the passage describing his meeting. Does "their briefest warbling sound" refer to the men in the meeting or to the rivers? Later in the paragraph he gains "a glimpse of them, inside" and notes that "they uncoil." Do "them" and "they" refer to the rivers or the others at the meeting? The syntax suggests the less challenging interpretation: these words refer to the rivers. Yet the ambiguity makes the passage more telling. Lyons's epigraph for this introductory chapter is from Emerson: "Every object rightly seen unlocks a quality of the soul." Perhaps, during the ordeal of his eight-hour meeting, even though spent in an unpleasant room with unpleasant others, he is able to see through those others to "Bright green live rivers." To carry this idea a bit further, Lyons seems to suggest that there is a hint of the majesty and wonder of the river to be found in the city and, later, that in the careful cultivation of knowledge on the river is to be found a wisdom that will enable one to live more fully and freely in the city.

Although rivers form the locus and the title of Lyons's book, he proceeds to explain the centrality of fish to the mental state derived from fishing that he values so highly. He describes a conversation with another member of his faculty who questions why he must fish in order to enjoy the rivers.

> It is difficult to explain but, yes, the fish make every bit of difference. They anchor and focus my eye, rivet my ear. . . . But fishing is *my* hinge, the "oiled ward" that opens a few of the mysteries for me. It is . . . especially so for fly-fishermen, who live closest to the seamless web of life in rivers. That shadow I am pursuing beneath the amber water is a hieroglyphic: I read its position, watch its relationship to a thousand other shadows, observe its steadiness and purpose. That shadow is a great glyph, connected to the darting swallow overhead; to that dancing cream caddis fly near the patch of alders; to the little cased caddis larva on the streambed; to the shell of the hatched stone fly on the rock; to the contours of the river, the velocity of the flow, the chemical composition and temperature of the water; to certain vegetable life called plankton that I cannot see; to the mill nine miles upstream and the reservoir into which the river flows—and, oh, a thousand other factors, fleeting and solid and telling as that shadow. Fishing makes me a student of all this—and a hunter. (1977, 15; emphasis Lyons's)

Again and again, Lyons repeats and restates this quality of fishing. He does not spend a great deal of time discussing the catch or even the missed catch. Instead, he explains as best he can the ineffable psychic effect that fishing has on him:

> Beyond the dreams and the theories, there are the days when a close friend will pick me up at dawn on my deserted city block and we will make the long drive together, talking, connected, uncoiling, until we reach our river for the day. It is a simple adventure we are undertaking; it is a break from the beetle-dull routine, a new start, an awakening of the senses, a pilgrimage. (17)

One wonders in reading this if the river can be read as not only a literal body of water but also as a state of mind or, more precisely, a state of relationship. Lyons describes himself as connecting to and entering into a relationship not only with the river but also with his fishing friend. As much as he speaks of his love of solitude when fishing, Lyons constantly describes his fishing with a friend. Time after time, he uses the word *connect*. On the river, he is connecting with another human and with his environment, whereas in the city he is unable, as far as he allows us to see, to connect either with the environment or, except in the fleeting moment during the business meeting, with other people. Later in *Bright Rivers*, Lyons makes a more specific iteration of the same principle: "You notice the weather more in the country. It has more of a direct link to your life. Everything is connected here. In the city, rain merely irritates" (66).

In *A Flyfisher's World*, Lyons once again visits the topic of solitude with a conflicted interest as he discusses popular fishing spots. "They're wonderful, I suppose, if you're selling something—from snake oil to books to religion to hard rock. . . . But have you ever heard a serious fly fisher sing their glory?" (1996, 230). He proceeds to detail the way in which the sport has exploded in popularity in the preceding decade, lamenting the passing of undervisited rivers, but opting for more exertion in the quest for solitude as the superior choice over trying to somehow diminish the crowds. Lyons is, after all, selling books, among other activities.

This concept of connectedness is explored by David James Duncan in *The River Why* when his protagonist, Gus Orviston, pens and soon puts into practice the "ideal schedule," which includes six hours of sleep, half an hour of eating "between casts or while plunking if possible," no school, fifteen minutes for bathing and bodily functions, thirty minutes for household chores, forty-five minutes for transportation, ninety minutes for tackle maintenance, and fourteen and a half hours for fishing (1983, 57–58). Gus, after a few months of living his ideal schedule, finds his life terribly unfulfilling. He realizes that he desperately needs to make connections. His first connection, an epiphany that would make James Joyce blush, comes when, drifting down the river on which he lives, he snags a drowned fisherman (94–97). In the aftermath of his traumatic encounter with the corpse, Gus begins to make connections with his neighbors: "I looked down the Tamanawis Valley. Pillars of blue smoke rose up here and there; beneath each pillar lived folks I'd never met, never sought out, never even greeted unless I had to. Whoever they were, they'd better watch out! A latter-day Piscator was about to attempt a little friendliness" (142).

What Gus Orviston realizes during the course of his novel, Lyons does not seem to consciously grasp in the pages of *Bright Rivers*. Throughout the book, Lyons speaks of his desire for solitude. He decries a shopping center that has been built where once there was a pleasant meadow (1977, 81). He speaks constantly of the connectedness of things and the lack of this value in the city. At the beginning of the "Far" section of the book, he tells the story of an altercation between a cabdriver and a pedestrian. The cabby calls the young man names, the young man batters the cab with a baseball bat, and people look on, with no sense of connection among them. Lyons describes the scene as being from a film and his attitude as "quite disembodied" (107–8).

Like those of Lyons, the stories of Thomas McGuane often demonstrate a sense of lack. While other fly-fishing writers seem to embrace their sport with an embarrassing enthusiasm, McGuane approaches the practice uncertainly. He is definitely an aficionado, but not one given to the myopic stripe that allows him to ignore his misgivings. Catching the most elusive species of fish for the fly fisherman simply elicits an "ecstatic resignation." Returning to the fishing waters of his youth forces him to acknowledge an unwelcome vein of sentiment in his normally cynical demeanor. Visiting the Golden Gate Club points out the impractical nature of his sport in a socially and ecologically challenged world.

Russell Chatham is another author who seems at once repelled and fascinated by modern society in all its questionable glory. In his 1976 story "No Wind in the Willows," Chatham, housebound by a Montana blizzard, tells a fishing story. His introduction to the story emphasizes both isolation and a merging with the crowd:

> Unable to go out, perhaps I will simply sit, reminisce and revisit. A word recurs, an idea, insisting upon the situation: remoteness. I moved to the Big Sky Country to get it. As an angler reflecting upon the fabric of American sport afield, I recognized the essential thread to be a romance with far places. In short, I'd identified the Mainstream and wanted in. (195)

Chatham tells a story of fishing in a strangely unpopulated San Francisco Bay area. His only brushes with humans in the story are with police officers and trustees of San Quentin prison, near which he stores a boat. During this trip, he catches a thirty-six pound, six-ounce, record-setting striper. "Getting his Polaroid camera, he [his fishing buddy, Frank] takes a picture of me holding the fish, which comes out a minute later looking distant and journalistic. Then after promising to call him as soon as I get the thing weighed, I head for San Rafael and he goes off to work in San Francisco" (203).

Chatham, a fine writer fully capable of expressing the impression of urban chaos, is presumably placing himself in this relatively barren setting for a reason. Similarly unusual is his ambivalent attitude toward the record he held. "Now others have caught bigger bass, eliminating my personal stake in the matter. It is a relief to be reminded that competition in angling is entirely beside the point and that I'm simply an angler of average persuasion and ability who happened to cast a fly near a large, hungry fish one morning" (204). In short, Chatham seems to find that having other humans involved with his fishing simply creates awkward situations.

The role of the connection to society in fly-fishing literature expresses itself in as many ways as there are writers. It can be found in Jack Curtis's "Grandfather" and the many other tales involving fathers or others teaching their sons or daughters to fish and through that tutelage to live. It is also evident in the dozens of expressions of environmental concern, both those that seem to despair over the state of the planet and those that look with admiration and hope at the positive impact of hunters and fishers upon wild places. Finally, it is found, as in the work of Nick Lyons noted above, as writer-anglers attempt to work out their own place in the world and thereby forge a relationship between their lives and the larger society.

As the mainstream of angling writers attempt to define their relation with a larger society, some might argue, with a good deal of validity, that such a definition does not require a huge effort. The typical angling writer is male and of British or, more rarely, German extraction. Their surnames tell the tale: Gordon, Haig-Brown, Lyons, Leeson, Harrison, Chatham, Duncan, Humphrey, and McGuane. They are such a homogenous lot that a name like Camuto stands out prominently. They are, as a rule, well educated and well heeled. Their inability to locate their proper place in the world will elicit little sympathy from many others whose births did not avail them of such privilege, and for the most part, those others remain silent in the field. There is no significant African-American fly-fishing literature. (I know of none at all.) Writers from economically disadvantaged backgrounds—Howell Raines being a prominent example—came to practice and write about fly fishing after becoming economically stable.

Despite the extent to which affluent white males dominate the field, one traditionally marginalized group, women, has produced a significant corpus of fly-fishing literature. While most of this work has been published only over the past twenty years, one should not forget that the first fishing book written in English is traditionally held to have been written by a woman. Indeed, a steady trickle of fishing writing by and about women runs through the middle of the American stream. The father of American fly-fishing himself, Theodore Gordon, argued for women's involvement in the sport: "I am surprised that more ladies do not take an interest in fly-fishing. It is well within their powers, and those accustomed to exercise soon become enthusiastic. Eight years ago a young lady was my fishing companion quite frequently, and although we had to tramp four or five miles to reach the best part of the river, she never became too tired to enjoy the sport" (92). This sentiment, expressed in an April 4, 1903, issue of *Field and Stream*, should be read in its context. Taken in its time, years before the suffrage movement achieved its goal, Gordon's statement was fairly revolutionary.

One of the first book-length contributions to the female fly-fishing tradition was Elsie Blackwood's *Many Rivers* (1968). In her first chapter, Blackwood tells of learning that her husband fished. "It was quite a shock to me six months after the honeymoon to discover that my husband owned fishing tackle" (14). After her husband had spent three successive and lengthening Sundays fishing with his friends, she determined not to be left out of his sport. Accompanying him on his next foray to the stream, Blackwood enjoyed her first fishing experience. Her husband agreed to bait her hook, since she had a problem with worms. She described the outing most poetically: "This is fishing: the golden sun; the green of the willows guarding the river bank, the busy life of the birds with their pulsing mad song. Were it not for these and the gentle ever-flowing river, time might stop" (23). Later, her description turns considerably more pedestrian: "Statistics show the [sic] more and more women are fishing each year. They stand braced against some current, their hands busy with the rod, eyes sparkling, while their brightly colored blouses and gay scarfs add a touch of flambuoyancy to the scene" (139).

If one were to apply Elaine Showalter's trichotomy, feminine/feminist/female, to the works under discussion, Blackwood's offering would definitely be classed in the category of feminine. While her book is a rather quaint call to the stream for American women, others who answered that call staked their claim to the waters in a more independent manner. In a sport as tradition-bound as fly fishing, it should not be surprising that relatively little writing that could be described as feminist has emerged. Mary S. Kuss offers one such work, describing her introduction to the sport. She tells of being tutored by a nearby doctor, who took her and his youngest son to the Beaverkill for two summers (1991, 64). It is easier to be a woman fly fisher these days than it used to be, she claims, since originally her appearance on a stream would "literally stop traffic. I'd hear a car screech to a halt on the road above me, someone would get out and stand at the guardrail and say something like, 'Jesus, Pete, would you look at this! It's a woman fly fishing! Now I've seen everything!'" (65).

In the category of distinctly female writing, one writer, while not dealing with fly fishing, deserves special consideration. Lorian Hemingway, the granddaughter of Ernest, produced a story, "The Young Woman and the Sea," that, while superficially just a fishing story, seems to relate the events of that fishing trip in distinctively female terms. The story begins as Lorian Hemingway expresses a desire to go and catch a marlin, partly to exorcise the ghost of her grandfather. Once out into deep water, she is strapped into a chair to fight the fish. The ensuing fight is described in a way that evokes images of a delivery room. The following passages give a flavor of that pattern of images:

> I could feel the pain in my back as soon as I hooked into him. . . . My muscles were cramping. . . . A wet towel had been put on my head. Then a bucket of sea water. . . . Douglas kept rubbing my cramped back. My head ached. I dearly wanted to see the thing that was sharing so much pain with me. . . . I let out a yell that made no sense. I screamed and pounded my right fist against my leg and heard all the other screams coming into chorus around me. (1991, 42–43)

After fifty-seven minutes of fighting this great fish, Lorian Hemingway's line breaks. In the moments after this ordeal, her companions attempt to comfort her. "'That's one big baby you just labored over,' I heard Dr. Engle say"(43). A short time later another fish is on the line. She describes this second attempt at landing the fish:

> Then the work was mine. Bloody, wrenching, brutal work. . . . Once again, the conversation evokes a delivery room. "What is it?" I hollered to no one in particular. "It's a blue, baby," Dr. Engle called back. . . . The talk was constant and beautiful. Everyone was with me. . . . And you *do* begin to love the fish because all the pain you are going through just to keep

him on the line is equal to the pain he feels in his attempts to lose the thing that has gripped him. (44–46; emphasis Hemingway's)

As the story reaches its climax, the obstetric imagery becomes ever more overt. The chair into which she is strapped takes on the image of a delivery table.

I was stretched flat-out in the chair. The back was down and I was holding onto the fish with everything I had left. And I was cursing Papa in my head. Just a good-luck curse is all. . . . "He's comin'! He's comin', boss. Comin' up!"

   . . .

"Reel! Damn it, Lorian, REEL!"
"I can't reel."
"YES, YOU CAN!"
"Lorian!" Hilary screamed. "Do you see him!"
"I see him Hilary!"

   . . .

"REEL! PULL! REEL! PULL!"
"You come down and fight him," I screamed. "I AM REELING!"
(46–47)

She ultimately brings the fish to the boat and releases it (48). Throughout this story, Hemingway's husband is a virtually impotent force. The captain and other fishermen serve like medical attendants, while Hilary, Lorian's sister-in-law, is the one most attuned to her struggle. No man has ever described the landing of a fish in any terms remotely like Hemingway's in this story.

While fly-fishing writing is still dominated by male perspectives, several women have managed to express their fishing experiences in a manner that is not dependent on or in response to the male viewpoint. Lin Sutherland tells of her initiation into the sport in a manner that might, with different pronouns, have been written by anyone. Joan Salvato Wulff, who has written a monthly column for *Fly Rod and Reel* since 1981, is similarly capable of demonstrating an ownership of her topic. Her words sound as self-assured as those of Ted Leeson, who describes the profound effect of being near a trout or salmon river. "Moving through the cool, clear water makes me a part of the river; and the act of casting connects me to what I see and feel with a grace and beauty of its own" (1994, 93).

From Great Britain, Lewis-Ann Garner expresses ideas that remind the reader of Nick Lyons and others who have followed in his manner: "For me there is no finer sport than fly fishing. It does not matter if I don't catch a fish. All that is important is that I am by the water's edge with my rod and nature as companions. Whenever a fishing holiday is over and it is time to leave, a part of me remains forever lost in that heathery mountainous wilderness" (1991, 154).

Ailm Travler brings not only a female voice to the discussion, but also one from the Native American tradition. Her words lend an especially personal style of the conversation ethic:

> Fly fishing twists fate like a dream and together with wildness, makes anything possible. Wilderness dances at the edge of nonsense and catastrophe. . . . Fly fishing both nurtures wildness and transforms it. . . . Fly fishing is a way of hooking into the world, being part of the swirling current and riffle patterns on a river, the tall grasses bending down into pocket water; the chill, the sun, the quiet or the screech of hawks. You become what you fish: a vulnerable cutthroat in a brushy, steep mountain stream; a sly brown hiding deep in the roiling waist-high waters of the Rio Grande. . . . Fly fishing is folly: useless, unreasonable, irrational, and without purpose. Fly fishing is folly precisely because it makes survival harder than it already is, and by doing so, turns survival into art. Like poetry, fly fishing is evocative beyond thought—the rings of water after a rise. Poetry may not be "useful," but its form obeys primordial laws of meter and rhythm. To utter the ineffable, one must retrace a journey to the beginning when meter and rhythm were born, the source of "a little language such as lovers use, words of one syllable" [V. Woolf, *The Waves*]. (1991, 207–8)

Where some female writers manage to forge an independent voice in a traditionally male genre, others explore one of the other areas of relationship commonly broached in fishing writing: family, and specifically parent-child relations. Le Anne Schreiber, in her essay "The Long Light," tells of moving to upstate New York to get into the sun and "bask." Her father brought her some fishing equipment, but since her memories of fishing were of long periods of enforced silence, she was unenthusiastic. At length, though, she began to fish. Her first success involved a treble-hooked lure that when swallowed killed "a very young, inexperienced, pink-finned brook trout. I watched it gasp and flap in my hand, watched its shimmering vibrancy turn dull and listless, then still and blacken" (1991, 6). Her father suggested that fly fishing was the answer to her dilemma. "Since my goal now was to imitate what hovers just above the water, I raised my sights a notch, taking in the air and light as well as the water they stir and dapple. My focus lengthened, as did the summer afternoons, which now extended well into evening before I even considered leaving the stream" (6). Fishing provided a common interest between father and daughter: "We were in league with the trout, allies in their progress from season to season, training them to fend off the harsher assaults of worm-danglers and hardware flingers" (7). The development of her fishing brought improvement in her relationship with her father. During this period, angling became their main topic of conversation. "Our phones seemed connected not by fiber optics but by the most delicately tapered of leaders, so sensitive that he felt the float of each fly, felt each slow swish of tail as the just-released trout steadied itself in the water before racing out of my loosely cupped hand. . . . The phone and mail flowed between us like a stream, rising to its highest level in late spring and tapering off to a trickle in the fall" (7). She sent him photographs of the places where she had caught fish. On her last visit to him, she found that he had kept the pictures at his bedside, "thumbworn at the corners" (8). During that visit, he showed her a number of things, including an old creel, that he wanted her to have after his passing (8). "This summer I will carry the creel, empty, and bear the wicker weight of his absence. They say death comes as an invitation to light. I hope so. I would like to think of life as a progress from light to light" (9). Schreiber here deals not only with her relationship with her father but also with her relationship to her own mortality.

Schreiber explores her other parental relationship in her memoir *Midstream: The Story of a Mother's Death and a Daughter's Renewal*, which treats her reaction to her mother's bout with pancreatic cancer. Gretchen

Legler, on the other hand, deals with the emotional economy of her entire family in her story "Fishergirl."

Mallory Burton, in her essay "Mentors," tells a tale of a much different sort of a father who did not understand fly fishing. Burton didn't have any mentors when it came to learning the sport, except for the minnows and other artifacts of her bait-fishing days. Her father couldn't understand why she would not use a minnow, but would spend hours studying the bugs on the surface of the water. At the end of Burton's essay, she relates a call from her father in which he told her that an old friend had left some fishing gear, including "wooden" rods behind when he died. Of course, the father didn't recognize the value of either the split-cane rods or the fly-fishing tradition they represented. In a second essay, "The Emerger," Burton revisits the parent-child relationship but this time takes the role of parent to herself. "I hoped, of course, that my son would eventually develop an interest in fly fishing, but I wasn't going to push him. Fly fishing isn't like that. Either it calls you or it doesn't" (1991a, 11).

In Burton's collection *Reading the Water,* the genders of her narrators become ambiguous or insignificant. In "Droppers" she relates the mental interplay between an excellent fishing guide and his client. Over the course of the story, the guide's advice is ignored and eventually proven correct, something that would evoke quite different responses if gender were foregrounded, yet it is entirely possible for a reader to finish this story without the client-narrator's gender coming into conscious thought.

Kathleen Dean Moore, although she mentions fishing only glancingly, must be numbered among those who appreciate the place of a river in the establishment of a sense of home and family. She begins her *Riverwalking* with a meditation on a daughter about leave home: "I wanted my daughter to lie in the tent, pressed between her brother and her father, breathing the air that flows from the Willamette River at night, dense with the smell of wet willows and river algae. . . . until the river ran in her veins and she could not help but come home again" (1995, 3).

Clearly, interpersonal relationships are a central concern of fly-fishing writing. Angling writers, in the course of creating their moments of time and space in the acts of fishing and then writing, make clearer the con-nections between self and society, but that is not the only connection these moments help to clarify. Another major area of interest is the con-nection between angler and nature.

It seems clear that for the angler the primary object for relationship in nature is the fish; thus it comes as little surprise that several writers have dealt with the connection between fisher and fish. There is, of course, a literal, physical connection involved in such a relationship. It is also, for the fish at least, potentially a life-and-death relationship. Ted Leeson sug-gests that in order to catch trout one must think not like a predator, as is commonly suggested by instructional works. Conversely, he argues that the successful trout angler will think like prey, causing the fly to behave as a creature that understands the value of escape and of insignificance. He notes that while the world of the predator is exciting, the world of the prey is much more like real life, as it is the prey and its elusiveness that re-ally control the world in which the predator exists (1994, 173).

While Leeson's claim that humans are more like prey than predator is rather difficult to completely accept, there do seem to be points of reso-nance between the fish and angler:

> Of one thing I am deeply convinced: if fish don't need us, we most cer-tainly need them. If a fish runs and jumps and shakes its head or dives into the weeds or wraps my line around a submerged log, or just bows its neck and bulls it out with me, then at least I know I've met a creature that wants its freedom as much as I want mine. Maybe that's why fishing should be a sacred act, an interaction with another creature that should never be taken lightly. (Quinnett 1994, 45)

Paul Quinnett finds in fishing the relationship with another freedom-loving creature. His is not a sport of dominance but of connection. In his article "Pavlov's Trout," Quinnett attempts a psychological analysis of the fascination that humans have with game fish.

> I have wondered whether it is the wildness in fish that somehow renews the wildness in us. After the hook is set and the shiver of something wild comes dancing up the rod, we seem somehow to be released from the

confines of our over-civilized selves. It is as if the fighting fish is the longed-for iron key that opens the golden door to our uncensored souls and what still might be wild in us. I have seen children squeal, women scream, and men bellow with delight at the first mad run of a just-hooked fish. I have heard their voices and my own ring out over a still lake. And in that instant, in that moment of abandonment to pure, uncluttered joy, there is, suddenly and momentarily, a brief glimpse into the untamed, unfettered, wild nature of what humankind once was, and what it still needs to be from time to time. (ibid.)

With fish as the central figure in the angler's relationship with nature, it should be noted that the river figures almost as prominently, if not more so. Certainly many works carry such titles as *Trout Magic* and *Trout*, but as many if not more carry names like *A River Never Sleeps*, *The Habit of Rivers*, and *A River Runs through It*. For Ted Leeson the river becomes a mystical thing that defies comprehension or domination.

A river . . . is only itself and has no way to resist being channeled into preconceptions or filtered through assumptions that falsify what it is. Come upon a river with purpose, or desire, or ideas, or even words and you merely make it into these things. We have overlooked countless rivers by seeing them just this way—that is, by not really seeing them at all. . . . Rivers also show a direction that is as well a misdirection. Taking our cues from the current, we regard their trajectory always downstream, and so look at them in reverse. Though they flow forward, rivers reach back, branching and rebranching between ridges, into the folds of hills, up to the tiniest valleys, back into crevices and creases, spreading at last between the grains of soil. Every square millimeter of earth is a watershed, and a river the most comprehensive expression of a landscape. (1994, 111)

Nick Lyons, like Leeson, sees the river as something that must be taken on its own terms. "Big rivers, little rivers," he begins. "Each has its own delights." There are no more good and bad rivers for Lyons than there are inherently good and bad people. The river, like a person, is not something to be controlled or improved, but simply to be met and known. "In the end, I guess the river doesn't quite make the man but the man seeks out the river to draw forth something in him. . . . And since most of us live

lives that are a bit too drab for the best inside us, and go to rivers to un-
lock much that lies dormant most of the year inside us, we like a variety of
waters" (1989, 176).

A good deal of fly-fishing literature is dedicated to a marking of the passage of time. Haig-Brown presents not only *Measure of the Year* but his four
books of the seasons. Nick Lyons chronicles the passage of a month on
Spring Creek in his book by the same name. Humphrey's novel *My Moby
Dick* is defined by the passage of a single trout season, with the urgency of
the impending death of the single legendary trout in an out-of-the-way
pool to add energy to the situation. For Howell Raines, the connection to
the calendar is of a wider scope, as the author traces himself through the
"mid-life crisis" during the book's course.

The true importance of time in fly-fishing writing emerges in works
such as those of Schreiber and Gallagher mentioned above, in which mortality and generational awareness are foregrounded. Such concerns figure
strongly in the work of Thomas McGuane as well. "Casting on a Sea of
Memories" takes McGuane back to a fishing site of his youth. Here, the
internal conflict is between his inclination toward sentimentality and that
toward "a universal irony." McGuane's normal tone is one of that universal irony, yet he acknowledges that this is a difficult one to maintain in
certain situations: "[W]hen you go back to a place where you spent many
hours of childhood, you find that some of it has become important, if not
actually numinous" (1988a, 13). The course of the story details the
difficult negotiation between these two tendencies. At one point, his self-
division is brought directly to the fore, as he loses a good fish: "with two
good bass for the night, I felt resigned to my loss. No I didn't" (17).

McGuane's trip to these home waters might suggest Hemingway's trip
to the Big Two-Hearted River or even Wordsworth's revisiting of Tintern
Abbey, yet this trip to Sakonnet Point winds its way on a path between
Hemingway's pragmatism and Wordsworth's romanticism. This middle
path seems to be McGuane's point in this essay, a point that he illustrates
in the final vignette in the text. McGuane describes how, during his childhood, a local fishing boat caught an uncommonly large ocean sunfish.

After landing the huge fish, the owners of the boat placed the carcass, bedded on a thick layer of ice, in an enclosed wagon, charging a dime to the local people who wished to see this mighty catch. Now, years later, McGuane describes coming upon the old wagon on his boyhood beach, still housing the skeleton of the great fish, evoking images of *The Old Man and the Sea*. This final image seems the perfect excuse for the numinous connection that he mentions at the outset of the essay, but rather than drawing any metaphysical connection, as would Wordsworth, McGuane casts an ambiguous attitude toward the sight: "If ever I opened an elevator door and found that skeleton on its floor, I would step in without comment, finding room for my feet between ribs, and press the button of my destination" (20).

McGuane describes a journey during which he seeks truth at least as actively as he seeks fish. Representative truth is also a prominent feature in the fiction of both Hemingway and Maclean. Fly-fishing literature, perhaps following the sport's preoccupation with the reproduction of nature, tends toward an almost classical privileging of mimesis. Whether that mimesis is found in the fly or on the printed page is irrelevant. Misdirections are common in nature, yet misdirection in words is quite another matter. Ted Leeson argues against the tendency to anthropomorphize the river. Fishermen realize, he claims, what many writers do not realize: "A river dances only in print, the author's trained monkey whose performance is unwitting and meaningless" (1994, 112). To so treat rivers or other natural things is to be untrue, Leeson argues. It is to impose ourselves on the natural. W. D. Wetherell in *Upland Stream* says that "the devaluation of words makes for a devaluation of the things words describe, and sets up a vicious circle from which there is no escape" (qtd. in Leeson 1994, 113).

The final connection, therefore, for the fly fisher, is to truth itself. All of the fly patterns, casting methods, entomological studies, and dozens of other minutiae are means to an end. The angler practices the various crafts of the sport—tying the fly, timing the cast, and reading the river—in order to create the ineffable moment. Lorian Hemingway, in "Walk on

Water for Me," describes the sport as a sacrament: "This is my body. Eat of it. This is my blood. Drink. I imagine this reverence is what they want of me" (1991, 37). Marjorie Sandor transforms the simple tale of a fishing trip to the Bitterroot River into a mystical spiritual quest worthy of Sir Gawain in "The Novitiate's Tale" (1996, 49). The completion of the process is to relate in words that speak with truth and power that same moment, a process that suggests Evelyn Underhill's definition of a mystic as someone who has gained an insight into the ultimate truth and managed to relate it back to others who have not ventured there (1990, 3–4). Buber describes this process as follows:

> The extended lines of relations meet in the eternal *Thou*. Every particular *Thou* is a glimpse through to the eternal *Thou*; by means of every particular *Thou* the primary word addresses the eternal *Thou*. Through this mediation of the *Thou* of all beings fulfilment, and non-fulfilment, of relations comes to them: the inborn *Thou* is realised in each relation and consummated in none. It is consummated only in the direct relation with the *Thou* that by its nature cannot become *It*. (75; italics in original)

Interlude 9

The Connection

WHEN I reached the low-water bridge over Crane Creek where the gravel road crossed the stream, I clambered out of the water and trudged back across a field to my car. A quick change of jeans and shoes later, I was in the car. Rather than driving back the way I came, I continued down the gravel road, passing under a trestle that bore up the old Missouri Pacific rails—now abandoned. After clearing the railroad, the road abruptly turned left, back toward town, so I thought it an acceptable risk to follow. A mile or so down the gravel, my faith was rewarded as the first signs of the town of Crane began to appear ahead of me. One of the first signs of civilization was a low concrete wall that curved out of the woods and passed close by the road before curving back into the woods. This, I was able to confirm in town, was the foundation of the old Crane roundhouse of the Missouri Pacific. Perfect had turned into magic, as two of my favorite things nestled into the same narrow Ozark valley.

The same old man who told me about the roundhouse asked me about the fishing. He was sitting on the stoop of a Casey's General Store, shooting a stream of tobacco juice to his right every minute or so. I was careful to stand to his left.

"So, did you have any luck?" he asked, abruptly changing the subject from trains to fish.

"Luck?"

"Luck. I assume you were up there fishing the creek!" he shot back.

I had known what he meant and for some vague reason had not wanted to acknowledge that I had been fishing. "I just had a couple of bites, but didn't catch anything."

He stared across the street to the garage for a good thirty seconds before talking again. "You go downstream from where the road crosses the creek about a quarter mile, and you'll find a big hole with a couple of sycamores growing on the west side. You try there, and you might have some luck." A smile oozed across his face, making me wonder if he wasn't just trying to send a city boy on a long walk.

"Thanks, maybe I'll give it a try."

In twenty minutes, I was walking down a narrow path that paralleled the stream on its east side. *Surely I've gone a quarter mile by now,* I thought to myself, and no sooner did I think that but a pair of white-and-gray sycamores burst into view across the water. The trees were magnificent, thrusting thick trunks up a good forty feet before sending branches in all directions. *If I were a trout, I'd want to live within sight of such trees.*

I laughed at myself for anthropomorphizing the fish, but then, looking at the water, I wondered if I shouldn't be laughing at myself for believing the advice of a strange old man. Where the water upstream had been glistening clear, this spot was cloudy, with dirt creeping up among the gravel. Still, I had walked this far; I might as well check out the fishing.

Assembling my rod, a skill I had gotten pretty quick at performing, I was leaning over the water seeking a place to cast in just a few moments. The pool was an oval, about fifteen feet across and thirty long. What struck me most, after my quick inspection, was that it seemed completely regular. There were no eddies, no fallen trees. There was nothing to suggest that any part of the water would be any better than any other. Where I had only suspected a trick before, I was now almost certain that the old man was sitting back on the porch and laughing at my expense while streaming tobacco onto the sidewalk.

With nowhere special to cast, I decided just to drop my fly into the middle of this puddle. I stripped off line and carefully checked for backcast room. I certainly didn't want to risk tangles or snags for this place. With all the fiddling and figuring out of the way, I could delay no longer. I drew my rod back and listened as the line swirled overhead. Just as it straightened out behind me, I pulled my hand forward, dragging rod, line, leader, and fly with it. The curve of the line straightened before my eyes. Releasing a little more line, I sent the rod backward once more, again feeling the weight of the line extend behind me. The line shot forward again as I rocked the rod back to the two o'clock position. The line fell gently onto the surface of the water. The leader then followed with the fly right behind, floating on its hackles. For a moment nothing happened, and I ripped the fly out of the water and recast, dropping the fly a few feet to the right. Nothing. Again and again, I cast, each time watching the fly strike a slightly different piece of water, each time getting a little angrier with the old man in town and with myself. Why would I ruin a perfectly enjoyable afternoon of fishing with a wild-goose chase for fish that I couldn't keep even if I did catch them? I cast again. Hadn't I grown beyond this? Didn't I know that there was more to fishing than catching fish? I cast again. Maybe I was no better than my brother-in-law the dangler. Maybe all I really cared about was conquest and dominance. I cast again.

The surface of the water exploded, and this time I did not hesitate to evaluate the situation. I just reacted, sweeping the rod back over my right shoulder and setting the hook. The line ripped to the left for ten feet and then reversed course to the right. After a few seconds of fury, I felt a moment of calm and began reeling in line gently. There were a couple of other bursts of energy, but after the first, there was never any real doubt that this fish was coming in. I drew the fish up to the bank, laid my rod down, and bent over to inspect my catch. I know it wasn't the proper thing to do, but I grasped it carefully and drew it out of the water to examine more closely. Unlike the beast of Taneycomo, this fish was not wounded in its mouth, nor were its fins ragged from rubbing against hatchery runway walls. This fish glowed in all the spectral glory one could desire. After carefully pulling the hook from its mouth, I laid my first rainbow back into the cloudy water. It paused for a moment above my open hands and then darted away. I watched its form, a shadow in the silty water, grow fainter until it faded into the depths.

It was a good drive home that night.

10

The View Downstream

TO this point, the current study has focused on issues that touch on the past and the present. The upstream forks of the subject belong to a rich and varied past. The reasons why people fish, the methods they employ to fish, and the connections they make while pursuing their sport are all concerns properly assigned to the present, yet they lead inexorably to a view of the future.

One might think it paradoxical to begin an examination of the vision of the future that underlies much of the literature of fly fishing with an examination of the sport's awareness of its past. It is perhaps overly obvious that, like most aspects of human endeavor, fly fishing has a long history, yet as has already been well documented, fly fishing is, probably more than any other pastime, heavily invested in its past. This awareness is significant, for an understanding of past tends to bring into prominence an awareness of future.

A great fishing tradition exists, stretching from Berners and Walton through Hemingway to a myriad of writers of the present. Fly fishing's attention to its history manifests itself in the awareness that anglers possess of standing in a great line that includes such luminaries as Theodore Gordon, Roderick Haig-Brown, Sparse Grey Hackle, and Norman Maclean. In North America, the tradition is not restricted to a traditional canon of writers and anglers, but continues back until it disappears in primordial mists. Thoreau describes such a connection with a prehistoric past in discussing the history of Walden Pond:

> An old man who used to frequent this pond nearly sixty years ago, when it was dark with surrounding forests, tells me that in those days he sometimes saw it all alive with ducks and other water fowl, and that there were many eagles about it. He came here a-fishing, and used an old log canoe which he found on the shore. It was made of two white-pine logs dug out and pinned together, and was cut off square at the ends. It was very clumsy, but lasted a great many years before it became waterlogged and perhaps sank to the bottom. He did not know whose it was; it belonged to the pond. (1977a, 439).

Norman Maclean closes *A River Runs through It* with a passage that traces fly fishing far beyond the lifetime of his father: "The river was cut by the world's great flood and runs over rocks from the basement of time. On some of the rocks are timeless raindrops. Under the rocks are the words, and some of the words are theirs" (104), a passage suggesting the primacy of the λογοσ in John's gospel.

While no other outdoor sport can trace such a distinguished pedigree in letters or practice over such a period of time as can fly fishing, a second manifestation of historical awareness is certainly not unique to nor even more prevalent in fly fishing. Like other outdoor sports the historical awareness of fly fishing is also expressed in a more informal manner with stories told and retold around campfires and coffee tables. The American literature of outdoor sport, including the fly-fishing writing considered here, while properly concerned with the present and the past, is perhaps most remarkable for its awareness of the future. This awareness is, of course, understandable. The fly fisher is potentially both a destroyer and a preserver of the wilderness. The sport's followers seem, more than others, to be conscious of their place in time, and their awareness of past brings about their sense of future.

One consistent theme, drawing on the awareness of both past and future, in not only the literature of fly fishing but that of hunting as well, is the idea of a long-past golden age. The manifestation of this sentiment ranges from the idea that there were more fish in the Beaverkill River two hundred years ago, to the road sign at the entrance of a fine fishing lodge in southern Missouri that reads, "You Should Have Been Here Yesterday! They Were Biting Like Crazy Yesterday!" The idea of the "good old days," while prevalent, is not always valid. While increasing numbers of anglers on most of the continent's waters have certainly had an effect on the populations of some species in some regions, in others the populations are greater than ever.

The ideal of a golden age, regardless of its validity, not only is popular in the literature and imaginations of anglers but has a considerable history, dating back to what may well be its first mention, in Hesiod's *Works and Days*:

> Far-seeing Zeus then made another race,
> The fifth, who live now on the fertile earth.
> I wish I were not of this race, that I
> Had died before, or had not yet been born.
> This is the race of iron. Now, by day,
> Men work and grieve unceasingly; by night,
> They waste away and die. The gods will give
> Harsh burdens, but will mingle in some good;
> Zeus will destroy this race of mortal men,
> When babies shall be born with greying hair.
> Father will have no common bond with son,
> Neither will guest with host, nor friend with friend;
> The brother-love of past days will be gone.
> Men will dishonour parents, who grow old
> Too quickly, and will blame and criticize
> With cruel words. (1973, 64)

Hesiod's sentiment is noteworthy for two reasons. First, it demonstrates the antiquity of the idea of the golden age, but more significantly, while not mentioning anglers, it seems to describe the mindset of a certain segment of the fishing world. Fishing, in general, is perceived to be a lot of work and hardship, with some good mingled in, but even with the good mingled in, there is still impending doom on the horizon. Just as Hesiod imagined a bleak end for human society (which some would say describes modern Western society fairly well), today's popular imagination envisions the end of the fisheries. Despite being born too late, though, Hesiod continues his treatise by instructing the doomed humans on how to maintain themselves by way of agriculture.

For Thoreau, the golden age was an age at least before his time—in the time of the Revolution, perhaps—and possibly a time before Europeans came to his country. He describes in *A Week on the Concord and Merrimack Rivers* first a decline in the fishing: "Salmon, shad, and alewives were formerly abundant here, and taken in weirs by the Indians, who taught this method to the whites, by whom they were used as food and as manure" (155). This statement might be taken as simply a factual one, which it probably was, but Thoreau's attitude and mood are more of interest here than the status of any species of fish. He foresees a possible return of these fish in centuries to come when nature has demolished the works of men.

Thoreau, in describing a degradation of the state of the natural world, parallels this decline with a decaying state of human culture. This should not be surprising, however, since in Transcendentalist philosophy these worlds are closely connected. In the following passage, it is poetry that is reaching an iron age:

> What a contrast between the stern and desolate poetry of Ossian, and that of Chaucer, and even of Shakespeare and Milton, much more of Dryden, and Pope, and Gray! Our summer of English poetry, like the Greek and Latin before it, seems well advanced towards its fall, and laden with the fruit and foliage of the season, with bright autumnal tints, but soon the winter will scatter its myriad clustering and shading leaves, and leave only a few desolate and fibrous boughs to sustain the snow and rime, and creak in the blasts of age. We cannot escape the impression that the Muse

has stooped a little in her flight, when we come to the literature of civilized eras. (Thoreau 1977b, 220)

More recently, Corey Ford acknowledges a bygone golden age while suggesting that the decline in the fish populations does not diminish the experience of the fishing:

> "The fishing isn't what it used to be," they tell you today. When I first fished the Beaverkill, over twenty-five years ago, they told me sadly: "The fishing nowadays isn't what it was." I suppose that when Hendrick Hudson sailed up to the Catskills, the Indians told him: "You should have discovered this place a hundred years ago. That's when the fishing was really good." It doesn't matter: a trout stream is more than the fish in it. A great trout stream like the Beaverkill is a legend, a fly book filled with memories, a part of the lives of all the devoted anglers, living or dead, who ever held a taut line in the current. (1990, 228)

Another echo of the golden age is found in H. Lea Lawrence, who describes the fishing in the Fox River, the probable prototype for Hemingway's Big Two-Hearted: "Fishing is still good in the river, but nothing like it was in 1919" (1992, 4).

Even the man-made trout paradise of Lake Taneycomo, in southern Missouri, has seen a marked decline in the four decades since the closing of Table Rock Dam. One writer contrasts his first trip to the lake with a more recent one:

> I shivered in the cold as lights from Table Rock Dam shown dimly through the dense fog. Four-thirty a.m. and already Lake Taneycomo regulars, fly fishers all, lined the hatchery outlet. Their casts punctuated the still, cold morning. Nothing had changed; yet everything had changed. Twenty-four years earlier, I'd stood in the same spot, lining an old fiberglass fly rod, tying on a shrimp imitation, preparing to fish Lake Taneycomo for the first time. That morning in the fog, I caught more large rainbows than I ever caught in my life; two exceeded six pounds. Nothing special for Taneycomo regulars back then. Bragging size started at seven and one-half pounds and went up. Ten pounders were common. (Turner 1994, 4)

Another writer complains that we "gobble up where-to articles in the sporting literature which extol the fishing in some spot that was productive a year or two ago but is dead today. 'Years ago' or 'the way it was' or 'I can remember when' crop up frequently in conversations" (Garrell 1993, 18).

This mood evokes images of a doomed Arthur continuing to preside over Camelot, of the Fisher King, and, more recently, of the star-crossed Paul Maclean from *A River Runs through It*, a master on the river, but unable to master life off the river. American fly-fishing writing, especially that which has endured best the passage of time, has within it, regardless of its generally positive tone, a sense of latent tragedy. For Nick in "Big Two-Hearted River," there is redemption only because of the specter of war behind him, and that specter cannot, at least yet, be completely shaken, as he cannot bring himself to fish the swamp. In the work of writers such as Howell Raines, that which haunts the fishing is the inevitable mortality waiting at the end of the line. For others it is the specter of ecological collapse that makes the day's fishing a divided pleasure.

In the past three decades, ecological awareness and concern for the environment have gone from being the province of fringe politics to the mainstream, culminating in George Bush's billing himself as the "environmental president." Environmental awareness, however, is not a new phenomenon. Thoreau, as described above, deplored the encroachment of human works on the river. More recently, Aldo Leopold brought a concern for conservation back into national awareness in *Sand County Almanac*. At the close of the twentieth century, the fly fisher is found right in the middle of the current debate over conservation, which centers on the question of who owns the resources of nature. For whose benefit are these resources to be employed? One side of this argument would assert that people have the right to use and dominate all parts of nature; the other side sees those on the first side as advocates of exploiting and destroying the land. Both of these parties, to some degree, would see the fly fisher on the wrong side of the argument, but perhaps both miss the point that the fly fisher understands.

Both the population that rolled across North America over the past three centuries, viewing the land as something to be exploited, and those who now see the land as something wholly separate from and requiring protection from human abuse have predominantly employed an *I-It* model of relationship. Robert Devine illustrates the prevailing attitude in his discussion of dams: "Dams epitomized progress, Yankee ingenuity, and humankind's impending triumph over nature. According to a children's book from the 1960s, we need dams to make rivers 'behave.' A 1965 Bureau of Reclamation booklet summed up the prevailing philosophy: 'Man serves God. But Nature serves Man'" (1995, 64).

Environmental writers, probably with some justification, examine recent patterns of consumption by contrasting them to a less destructive age. Calvin Martin, discussing Native American attitudes toward hunting and fishing, claims that "once upon a time man and animals talked with one another on this continent. Why they ceased their conversation is a question for the ethnohistorian to ponder; whether they will ever do so again is a question for the prophets" (1978, 156). Just as early Hollywood films tended to treat Native Americans as savages, recent offerings have adopted an attitude similar to Martin's, viewing the Native American as a pinnacle of environmental awareness from which, with the continued influx of Europeans, North America has fallen. Thoreau follows this pattern, detailing the degeneration of fishermen in a manner similar to that employed by Hesiod in describing the descent from the Golden Age, finally portraying an angler whose provisions featured rum most prominently.

Thoreau, however, like many in and near the fly-fishing tradition, did not view this descent as an irredeemable tragedy. Unlike Hesiod, who wrings his hands over the passing of the Golden Age and counsels his reader simply to make do in the present, Thoreau locates his Golden Age in a more recent past and is thus able to urge the reader to attempt to live according to Golden Age values, employed in a Golden Age vocation.

> In defending the vocation of the Golden Age, Thoreau was defending his own: the villager and the Walden experimenter were already projected, the specialized and the whole man, the man cut off from and the man within the tides of life. In the image of the fisherman and the judge were

all the values of Whitman's "When I Heard the Learn'd Astronomer," the belief in knowledge by contact and communion, the vitalistic idea of a living world, in which fish and water, thought and flux were one, and in which the goal of living intensely was by the meeting with this flux at its creative moment, when by immersion in it one shared the "spirit." It was in this sense that the fisherman represented Thoreau's vocation: he would get his living, like the colonists of Concord, from nature—and his life. (Paul 1972, 215)

Accepting the vocation of the Golden Age is attractive when that vocation remains a hazy ideal, yet when applied to the specific conditions of present and future, it becomes more complicated. What are the behaviors that one who has embraced the Golden Age vocation should exhibit? Just as a religious devotee, having accepted certain doctrine will be expected to behave in an appropriate manner, the fly angler can be expected to embrace certain values and qualities. The attitudes described in the preceding chapters might be rightly assigned to this list of values and qualities, yet there is an additional attitude that relates especially to the future, the sense of the proper (I-Thou) relationship between humans and nature.

As has been evidenced in the works of Thoreau, such a relationship is not a completely new idea to the American scene. More recently, and more specifically oriented toward outdoor sport, are the attitudes represented in the writings of Theodore Roosevelt, who wrote mostly about hunting; yet the attitudes he espoused before, during, and after his tenure in the White House are found prominently in the fly-fishing writing that came in the years after. Roosevelt is most commonly associated with the Panama Canal and San Juan Hill and is thus perceived as an imperialist and a conqueror. To portray Roosevelt in such a manner, however, is to misunderstand and stereotype him. The most notable value informing Roosevelt's opinions is the belief that natural resources are not to be owned or conquered. They are, in Roosevelt's view, more closely akin to cultural treasures: poetry, theater, or language itself.

Surely our people do not understand even yet the rich heritage that is theirs. There can be nothing in the world more beautiful than the Yosemite, the groves of giant sequoias and redwoods, the Canyon of the

Colorado, the Canyon of the Yellowstone, the Three Tetons; and our people should see to it that they are preserved for their children and their children's children forever, with their majestic beauty all unmarred. (1990, 317)

His view on game did not extend as far as current laws, which provide government control over all game, yet it was relatively intrusive for the time: "Most emphatically wild game not on private property *does* belong to the people, and the only way in which the people can secure their ownership is by protecting it in the interest of all against the vandal few" (253; emphasis Roosevelt's). This opinion can probably be traced to his observation concerning big game: "The most striking and melancholy feature in connection with American big game is the rapidity with which it has vanished" (287).

Extending his philosophy to an activity he knew intimately, Roosevelt offers considerable opinion concerning the taking of game. His most obvious observation is that hunting must be done in what would now be termed a sportsmanlike manner. The true sportsman, he argues, is not a threat to continuing populations of wildlife:

> True sportsmen, worthy of the name, men who shoot only in season and in moderation, do no harm whatever to game. The most objectionable of all game destroyers is, of course, the kind of game butcher who simply kills for the sake of the record of slaughter, who leaves deer and ducks and prairie-chickens to rot after he has slain them. Such a man is wholly obnoxious; and, indeed, so is any man who shoots for the purpose of establishing a record of the amount of game killed. (1990, 290–91)

Roosevelt, while arguing strongly for the rights of temperate taking of wildlife, could by no stretch of the imagination be described as guilty of bloodlust. In fact, he relegates the kill to a subordinate role in his hunting: "As we grow older I think most of us become less keen about that part of the hunt which consists in the killing. I know that as far as I am concerned I have long gone past the stage when the chief end of a hunting trip was the bag" (253).

One final aspect of Roosevelt's conservation ethos is his sense of balance. "There is much to be said for the life of a professional hunter in lonely lands; but the man able to be something more, should be that something more—an explorer, a naturalist, or else a man who makes his hunting trips merely delightful interludes in his life work" (336). Most hunters (and, presumably, fishers) should aspire to be something more than simply game killers. He goes on to argue that "if sport is made an end instead of a means, it is better to avoid it altogether" (337).

Roosevelt can be credited with creating a forward-looking conservation spirit in the United States. Following his lead, American outdoor writers have discovered that "it is an incalculable added pleasure to any one's sum of happiness if he or she grows to know, even slightly and imperfectly, how to read and enjoy the wonder-book of nature. All hunters should be nature lovers" (339).

The forward-looking ember that Roosevelt kindled has been fanned into flame by the writers of the last half of the twentieth century. These writers, faced with dwindling populations of fish pressured by growing numbers of anglers, attempting to live and reproduce in polluted and structurally altered habitats, find their sport to represent a paradox. Anglers represent consumption and destruction, yet they, at the same time, attempt to stand for preservation and restoration. William McLarney, in his "Who Says They Don't Make Trout Streams Anymore?" describes a decades-long effort by anglers to restore the fishing opportunities in Cape Cod, a site that has probably been fished for more years than anywhere else in the United States.

The same paradox is noted by Barry Lopez when he discusses the management of geese in the United States: "We preserve them, principally, to hunt them" (1989, 31). This is, perhaps, an overstatement, as certainly many in the various government agencies that concern themselves with the well-being and futures of various species are equally interested in biodiversity and the inherent beauty of the creatures being preserved. Nevertheless, there is enough of a kernel of truth in Lopez's statement that it must be considered. Across the nation, there are numerous trout hatcheries whose sole purpose is to maintain a large population of fish for anglers to catch. The state of Missouri, for example, maintains four state parks dedicated largely to hatchery trout fishing. In these parks, which draw as many as a half-million visitors per year, the Department of Conservation stocks the waters each day with roughly three times the number of fish as anglers expected the next day (Tryon 1992, 10–11). These fish are not just preserved to be caught but are actually bred and raised for this purpose. In a less extreme case, hatcheries all over the United States, Canada, and the United Kingdom maintain the trout population in overpressured streams and rivers. It is said that many trout anglers simply follow the hatchery trucks for a good day on the stream. "Many wild-trout advocates disdain hatchery fish precisely because these fish are too stupid to protect themselves and stupid fish do not make good sport" (Quinnett 1994, 45).

Aware of such situations, many anglers seek to protect nature more carefully than the law requires. Haig-Brown, writing at a time when legal limits on game were fairly lenient and new, expressed his attitude as follows: "I think the wise fisherman, who knows what is good for the present and future of his sport, usually pays little attention to the size limits or the bag limits allowed by most game commissions" (1975b, 64).

Nick Lyons, fishing Spring Creek, values that resource highly enough to restrict his methods. The creek, he says, was a perfect dry-fly creek; thus he limited himself to dry flies when fishing there. "Besides, it seemed part of the stewardship of the resource to grant the trout all the water below the surface, to fish a bit less, to key the whole experience to that place where water and air meet" (1989, 95).

One widely popular outgrowth of the forward-looking attitude is the catch-and-release ethic. For many fly fishers, killing a trout is simply unthinkable. Most others put back at least some of the legal fish that they catch. Not only is catch-and-release seen as a prudent conservation method, but it takes on an almost spiritual quality. One angler describes his catch-and-release experience as follows: "I released that fish and it quickly swam away. I had read about catch and release, but as an old southern bass fisherman, I couldn't imagine how anyone could spend all that energy catching a fish and then put it back in the water—that is, until I saw the trout. Once again, the aesthetic impulse prevailed" (Norman 1987, 55). Robert Traver, on the other hand, though he admires such "poetic dilations like this from the great-hearted giants among fishermen, and each time I get a powerful big lump in my throat" (123), nevertheless confesses that when he catches a big fish, he tends to keep it. "My really big fish are few and far between and I keep them. Furthermore, I wail like a banshee whenever I lose one" (1989, 124).

While catch-and-release's history can be traced back to Lee Wulff's 1938 book *Handbook of Freshwater Fishing*, its future seems bound to spread to many non-fly-fishing methods. Howell Raines describes how Ray Scott, the founder of B.A.S.S. (Bass Anglers Sportsman Society), has popularized catch-and-release among the vast numbers of bass anglers:

> The catch-and-release gospel spread quickly enough among warm-water fishermen to force makers of bass tackle to drop their historical practice of advertising lures by showing a stringer of dead fish. Editors of saltwater publications got angry letters for pictures of fish being landed with a killing stroke of the gaff. All up and down the East Coast, guides like Mark Kovach on the Potomac and Bob Clouser on the Susquehanna altered their policies of allowing a customer to keep one or two trophy fish and went to complete no-kill fishing. (1994, 176)

Martin Garrell also notes the spread of the catch-and-release practice from fly fishing into other areas of the sport:

> The ethic of catch-and-release, championed decades ago by anglers like Lee Wulff, has spread widely across the saltwater scene. The statement that "A good fish is too valuable to catch only once" has spread from salmonids, billfish, tarpon, and bonefish across the entire spectrum of angling. . . . For the next generation, quantity and size, even for inshore species, may no longer be the principal measures of fishing experience, but the quality of recreational fishing should still be substantial, thanks to education and a conservation ethic. (1993, 19)

As important to the sport as catch-and-release has become, it is not the only effect that the forward-looking orientation has brought about. Underlying the philosophy of catch-and-release and other conservation-minded practices one finds an orientation that has, within the past century, tended away from consumption and domination and toward preservation and creation. Harmon Henkin, certainly not a stereotypical fishing guide or writer, is drawn to what he perceives to be an entirely new type of angler. After describing a morning's conversation between a fly-fishing guide and his "youngish and enlightened" clients, Henkin bursts into the narrative with a strident aside: "Sexism! Imperialism! Ecology! Scarcely the basic concerns of earlier generations of fishing guides, who were mostly concerned with getting their customers into fish and keeping them out of danger" (1988, 106–7). Curiously, however, as advanced as these anglers might be seen to be, they still find themselves drawn to the tradition of fly fishing.

In his book *Many Rivers to Cross*, M. R. Montgomery describes catching a trout in the upper reaches of the Rio Grande. It is a nice-sized fish, but, he notes, it bears too many speckles to be a native brook trout. Upon closer examination, he discovers the telltale rainbow-hued lateral stripe that betrays hybridization (1995, 123). Anglers at the end of the twentieth century, especially in North America, are similarly hybrid. While employing methods that reach back over decades and centuries, these anglers employ new technology at a far greater level than practitioners of any other sport. The World Wide Web provides access to well over 300 sites dealing in some way with fly fishing. Internet mail lists and Usenet newsgroups generate over a hundred messages a day.

The dividedness that accompanies the attempt to focus both on the tradition of the past and the promise of the future, underscores the essential quality and underlying purpose that has been carved out for fly fishing within modern culture. The fly angler seeks to forge connections with past and future. They are sought with nature and other humans. Most obviously, they are sought with the fish that lurk beneath the water's surface. The end result of these ties, however, brings with them the ultimate paradox of fly fishing. The product of these myriad relationships is not connection but separation. More precisely, the angler, by means of clearly establishing his or her relationship with the world, creates and defines a present, a personal space, and a clearer self-knowledge.

Aftermath

I PROMISED *Olivia I would take her fishing. I didn't promise that it would be fly fishing, although after catching that rainbow at Crane Creek, I wanted nothing more than to get a fly rod into each of my children's hands. Olivia, however, was only two and a half. That seemed a bit early to be fly fishing, so I opted for the old faithful: worms and a Zebco baitcaster for bluegill.*

We cast her first line off the side of my brother's dock at the Lake of the Ozarks. The line sported a small hook impaling a night crawler. Above the hook, I had strung a split-shot weight and a bobber.

"When you see the ball go in the water, then you have a fish," I advised her. "Do you understand?"

She nodded and watched the bobber. Within seconds a cloud of bluegill hovered near the hook.

"Do you see the fish?" I asked her. She didn't answer, but the intent look on her face suggested that she did indeed see the fish.

After a brief wait, one of the fish became bold enough to make a move for the worm. The bobber quivered, danced, and then plunged into the water.

"You've got one, Livy!" I shouted, startling her. "Pull back!"

She watched the bobber run deep and then float back to the surface. Reeling in, I found the hook picked clean. After rebaiting her hook, we tossed the rig in once again. Within seconds the bobber was again streaking down and away from us.

"Okay, Livy," I said. "Pull back and catch him!" This time I pulled back with her. My hands on top of her hands, I felt the shudder in the rod that the hooked fish transmitted. As bluegill are wont to do, this one put up a worthy fight, but before long it was plopped unceremoniously into a minnow bucket full of water on the dock. Olivia was content simply to sit cross-legged beside the bucket for quite a while watching her fish, but eventually she came back to the rod long enough to put another into the bucket.

It was about this time that Emily and Alyson, aged eleven and ten, stomped onto the dock. They admired Olivia's fish and watched us for a moment as we tried to add number three.

"Dad," Emily asked. "Can I fish?"

"Me too!" Alyson chimed in.

I gave them a dozen worms and pointed them toward a couple of rods, but by the time Olivia had tired of the game, neither of the others had gotten a line into the water. Alyson was disgusted by the idea of hooking a worm, and Emily wasn't too keen on the whole thing. Neither of them knew how to rig up the combination of bobber, weight, and baited hook, and that was when the realization pierced me like a sharpened hook. I had never really fished with them.

I had taken Emily when she was a little older than Olivia. I had never taken Alyson. The best we had ever done was to rifle through my tackle box on a winter night, but we had never fished together.

It took only a few minutes to rig each of them up properly. Emily, teeth gritted, baited her own hook, but Alyson allowed me to do the honors. As the sun began to slink down toward the horizon, we plopped two lines in the water and waited. It took only a moment for Emily's bobber to streak downward. Instinctively, like she does nearly everything, she jerked back at the perfect moment. Seconds later she tossed a flopping six-inch bluegill onto the planks of the dock. I extracted the hook, and we flung the catch back into the water.

By this time, Alyson was getting some action, but she, like she does most everything, jerked at exactly the wrong time, and the fish disappeared. We repeated this dance a half-dozen times. It took no time for Alyson to get another bite, but each time she either yanked back immediately, sending hook and bobber alike flying back into our faces, or she waited too long, allowing the fish to feel the hook and spit it out.

As shadows lengthened, I feared that we wouldn't get Aly a fish that night. Emily, meanwhile, had landed and returned four or five, although none was worth bragging about.

Penny stepped out onto the deck above us just as Emily drew another quivering fish from the lake. As I gripped the fish around the belly and extricated the hook, I saw Alyson's bobber plunge again beneath the water. Tossing Emily's fish back, I focused on Alyson.

"Wait, Aly!" I cautioned, hovering just over her shoulder. "Not yet." The bobber ran a little deeper. "Now!" I yelled.

Dutifully, she yanked back. The immediate dance of the line made it clear that the hook was in. "Do I have it?" she shrieked.

"You've got it! Reel in!"

The fish that emerged from the water that night was scarcely big enough to grab her hook, but she didn't seem to mind. The moment the fish was off the hook and back in the water, she insisted that I rebait her hook.

The bluegill kept biting that night for as long as we had light. For as long as we had light, I sat between my daughters, baiting their hooks and freeing their fish. The sun sank behind the ridge on the west side of the cove, dappling the water in bronze and lead. No longer could we see the shadowy outlines of the fish hanging in the water, but we felt their tugs on the line and we reeled them up out of the murky depths, confronted them, and then tossed them back to be caught again. Again I baited a hook and felt that moment of joy as another fish emerged from the water. I sat there on the dock with them fishing as the last vestiges of light faded away too soon.

II

Rivers to the Sea

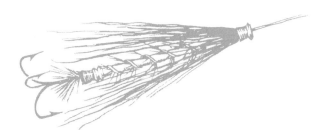

THE connection between the compulsion to fish and the compulsion to write about fishing has been noted by both those within and those without the tradition of fly-fishing literature. Nick Lyons states the issues very clearly:

> In the best stories about fly fishing—by Norman Maclean, Roderick Haig-Brown, Robert Traver, Sparse Grey Hackle, William Humphrey, Howard Walden, and ten thousand others who tell them in camps and at lunch tables but do not write—we find the best clues to why some of us fish. Odd, funny things happen; there is mystery and suspense, challenge and discovery; the words have the warm colors of earth and water, not the jargon of the specialist; we meet real people, with warts and wit and maverick gestures; big fish are caught or lost; people say wild and spontaneous words; event becomes memory and sometimes, in the hands of a master, bleeds into art. (1989, 18)

The reasons, as Lyons describes them, are not simply enumerated in those oral and written stories. Instead, the stories are, to some degree at least, the reasons themselves. While Nick Lyons might fish even if he had no one to read his fishing tales, he would probably fish differently. For Lyons and others who do not state the condition quite so overtly, the boundaries between the fishing and the writing are difficult to draw.

The fly fisher seems compelled to write. Shelves at any of hundreds of tiny local fly shops will strain under the weight of dozens if not hundreds of titles. On the other hand, at the self-proclaimed "World's Largest Sporting Goods Store," the cavernous Bass Pro Shops in Springfield, Missouri, which sports every bass lure imaginable, there are only a handful of books on bass fishing to be found.

One might wonder how much can be profitably written about even so complex a subject as fly fishing. The Library of Congress records over four hundred new titles cataloged under the main heading of "fly fishing" since 1977. This figure does not reflect the hundreds of titles cataloged under myriad subheadings.

Nick Lyons, describing the increased interest in the sport, notes the increase in the number of books published, "some of which sell in numbers not previously imagined—while other decent ones vanish simply because there are too many titles vying for attention" (1996, 231). Clearly, it would seem, publishers have continued to find that a great deal can be profitably written on the subject, yet many of these publications must be categorized as what David James Duncan's character Jeremiah Ransom calls "redumbdancies": "Jeremiah speculates that were the nation's Top Ten fishing writers to swap jobs with, say, the Top Ten basketball reporters, NCAA and NBA coverage would suddenly scintillate with headlines like 'How to Handle Those Pesky New Velcro Shoe-Fasteners,' 'Ten Ways in Which Tall, Fast Players Are Preferable to Short, Slow Ones,' 'Some Advantages of Outscoring the Opponent' and so on" (Duncan 1995, 164). While there is certainly truth in Jeremiah's opinions, what is more intriguing is the repetitive nature of the reflective writing about fishing and its continued popularity. The more literary expressions of fishing writing make no claim to be breaking new ground. They might be compared to the seemingly endless musical settings of the more popular Psalms. One writer even uses the metaphor of the hymnody, suggesting that "every book about fishing ever published is materially a book singing its praise, however poorly or well the author sings the song. The songs of angling praise are few in number, but they come in countless thousands with different words to the same beguiling tunes" (Hammond 1994, 226). Fishing writing, viewed in this light, can be seen as almost a catechism or litany. All involved come to the words fully aware that nothing new is forthcoming, yet remain faithfully attendant to their repetition and variation.

Nick Lyons is fascinated by the mystery of this eruption of words:

> Probably none of it will make you a better fly fisherman, anyway—and any novel by Hardy, Melville, Waugh, Dickens, Tolstoy, Dostoyevski, Sterne, Proust, Joyce, Hemingway, Marquez, Faulkner, or Jane Austen is better worth your time. These [novelists] will make you a wiser human being, which has a good chance of making you a wiser fly fisherman. But don't count on it. (1977, 112)

Bryn Hammond, early in his study of the culture of trout fishing, continues this thought:

> Someone once remarked that the quality of fishing writing—that is its quality as literature—varied inversely to the quality of the fishing. That is not totally unlike suggesting that sackcloth and ashes and suffering provide a better path to the kingdom of heaven than the comfort of all the riches of this world. But I don't really believe it to be true. The United States has long provided some of the very best and most taxing fly fishing in the world, often with an intelligent sort of purity of purpose about it; not a blind adherence to outmoded cults. The United States has also produced much of the finest reflective fishing writing of all time, particularly on the question of why men fish. (1994, 9–10)

Hammond is drawn not just to the quality of American fishing writing, but to the question of why this writing exhibits this quality. He explores this question, without arriving at any real answer in the following passage:

> Why should it be that American writers have come closer to describing what virtually all addicted fishermen know and experience about those "uncommonly difficult to explain" things than writers from other parts of the world? Is it because they have greater sensitivities about such matter?

Is it because they are often better, not necessarily as anglers, but as complete anglers? Is it because Americans are less inhibited about what they really feel, and in no way embarrassed about describing and sharing those feelings? Of one thing I am certain. Whether or not any reader now knows any more about why men fish I can have no gleaning. But should any reader not have felt that old tingling, that old response, in reading these words, and have not had similar awareness at times—even fleetingly—then he has not yet traveled far enough along the road towards his own angling Damascus. (16)

The manner in which Hammond describes fishing could easily be applied to a description of writing. Hammond seems to be fascinated by the question of why humans feel compelled to fish, while at the same time he appears to border on despair at the possibility of arriving at an answer. At his most optimistic, Hammond mysticizes fishing, likening the understanding that a true angler enjoys to Saint Paul's awakening on the road to Damascus. In short, Hammond seems to suggest, despite the compulsion that anglers feel toward writing and retelling their fishing experiences, there can be no verbal answer to this question of why people fish. Similarly, it might be said that there is no verbal answer as to why writers write. The answers can only be found in the fishing and the writing respectively.

While everyone would agree that writing is a creative act, some might find it odd to consider fishing in the same manner. Properly approached, however, fishing is capable of leading not just to the catching of fish, but to an act of creation, yielding a moment of transcendent quality, insight, self-knowledge, or other benefit. Fly-fishing writers, who are, admittedly, not disinterested, would argue that the proper approach to fishing is fly fishing. While various reasons can be used to explain the wealth of writing on the subject, several of the angling writers themselves suggest, either directly or indirectly, that the moment produced by proper fishing is a moment much like that produced by quality writing.

In the preface to his *Confessions of a Fly Fishing Addict*, Nick Lyons describes the misgivings that he experienced when undertaking a monthly column. He worried that he could not pour all of himself into the short form, but found that focus on the limited bounds of the column, like the focus on a limited stretch of water, yielded rich results. Lyons proceeds to assign fishing to a role more as catalyst than active agent in the production of fishing literature. "Many of the best fish tales only begin with the fish" (1989, 18). Continuing, he seems to simultaneously undermine and build up the literature of fishing.

> There is some lunacy in it all—and some playing Huck Finn, to regain our childhood. But that lunacy and those images are specks of sand that, like the sand in an oyster, become a fisherman's pearls. Some are funny jewels, some sad, and some touch our hearts. All are part of the great storehouse of memories and tales that make up a fisherman's quirky and crammed brain, keeping us gut-hooked from one season through the long gray winters until another season starts. (20)

It is not at all clear, either from Lyons's discussion or from the literature itself, where this "gut-hooking" has its base, in the fishing or in the words that grow out of the experience. In some ways it seems that each depends on the other for its nurturance.

One of the most notable aspects of much fly-fishing and its attendant writing is that in its relentless creation and redefinition of connections, a terrific blurring of boundaries is achieved. Norman Maclean's celebrated opening for *A River Runs through It* declares, "In our family, there was no clear line between religion and fly fishing" (1976, 1). Similarly, in inspecting the literature of the field, the dividing lines blur between the art and the craft, between the fishing and the writing, and between fact and fiction.

Fly fishing, for its most devoted apologists, is as much an art as poetry: "Few game fish have received as much attention from artists and poets as the trout. But beyond their aesthetic appeal, creatures like this brook trout challenge the skills of anglers. Today, the sport of trout fishing is an art in itself" (Norman 1987, 53). Even if one finds such a statement excessive, there can be little argument that fly fishing is looked upon as among the most poetic of sports. Geoffrey Norman underscores this perception in a tone that seems mostly serious: "A poet sent me to my first trout stream. At the time, I found that a little quaint. But as I look back on the experience, I can't imagine a more appropriate guide. After all, it was an aesthetic impulse rather than a sporting urge that inspired me to go trout fishing in the first place" (54).

Writing at its best, like fishing at its best, is an act of the imagination. "Thus to the writer, fishing and imagination become kin, if not identical twins, and like Moby Dick in the mind of Captain Ahab, the challenge need be honored to bring out the dimensions of men" (Curtis 1988, 48). Jack Curtis's story "Grandfather," while dealing with the relationship between the generations, also makes the connection between fishing and the life of the mind. The reason that Curtis leaves the home of his father in this story in order to live with his rather disreputable grandfather is due to poor performance in school. Like a skilled rhetorician, the grandfather manages to use fishing to bring his grandson into an appreciation of where reading and writing might take him.

The actions of Jack Curtis's grandfather concern fishing, yet they do not concern fishing alone. Such complexity enshrouded in simplicity is a quality of many fishing tales. "Big Two-Hearted River" appears to be simply the story of a solitary fishing trip, but it is not that simple. *The Compleat Angler* is apparently just a dialogue concerning methods of fishing, yet it is more. Jim Harrison touches on this tendency in his appraisal of the best of outdoor writing as that which exists "on the periphery of sport. . . . These writers are first of all artists and they deliberately avoid even a tinge of fakery" (1988, 168).

Probably the most prominent fly-fishing narrative after (or perhaps even before) Hemingway is Maclean's *A River Runs through It*. The fishing is what people remember from the novella, yet it serves more as a fulcrum than as a true topic for the writer. Throughout the story, the reader is accompanied with the nagging feeling that this is a tale about fishing and yet not just a fishing tale. Even in the end, with Paul's violent death reported with journalistic detachment, the reason for the work remains as murky as the reasons why the brothers fish. Clearly Norman does not accept his father's metaphysical explanations of fishing, nor is he his brother's equal with a fly rod, yet Norman, early in the novella, says with a tinge of regret, "It is true that we didn't often fish together anymore" (9). Norman seems to fish, after the manner of his father, simply because he always has. Paul, while the more accomplished angler, shows no more knowledge of why he journeys to the river than of why he gambles to excess. Fishing, for the brothers, is an unexamined artifact in their lives.

Curiously, one critic sees Maclean's novella as a textual artifact of the same sort:

> Fourteen years after publication, Norman Maclean's A River Runs Through It and Other Stories cannot be read, only re-read. Few come to the work unaware that this is the stuff of legends. . . . Readers are predisposed to see the title story . . . as the story of Norman Maclean, as an accouterment to the legend, and thereby fail to engage the writing. "A River" is no longer art but an artifact, a totem for the myth of Maclean. (Hammond 1994, 263)

A River is a paradox in itself. It argues against the conventions of writing. Weighing in at 104 pages, it is shorter than a novel, but too long for a short story. While highly autobiographical, it clearly reads like a novel, making its categorization as fiction problematic. The driving conflict of the story is not really clear until the last few pages, if one can really say that is clear at that point. The several critics who have attempted comment on the work seem to find it difficult to catch hold of the text. Virtually every study of A River quotes the memorable opening—"there was no clear line between religion and fly fishing"—or the equally marvelous ending—"I am haunted by waters"—but beginnings and endings are natural and easy places to engage a text. Together, these two passages represent only a tiny fraction of the entire work, yet they seem to receive virtually all the attention, probably because the critics have no certain idea of what to do with the remaining pages. Publishers were not certain what to do with Maclean's work, either, and only when the University of Chicago Press, which had never before published a work of original fiction, took a chance on the manuscript did the book appear and then sell over 160,000 copies with virtually no advertising.

Like A River Runs through It, fly fishing itself is a difficult text to read, replete with ironies and paradoxes. Ted Leeson finds a narrative form not just in the sport's writing, but in the ironies of the sport itself:

The ironies are delightful. The grossest and most substantial of our equipment exists solely to serve the slightest; a thousand dollars' worth of gear is given meaning by a quarter's worth of chicken feather and wire. . . . All is focused on the ultimately crude reenactment of an event that happens a million times a minute in the natural world. Nature is the most exacting of models, and in fly fishing nothing hints more emphatically that we are on the right track than the difficulty of our labors. These ironies and their grand disproportion give fly fishing a distinct form. Grosser things serving finer ones, the clumsy and tangled labor for the ordinary, the consequential hinging on the apparently slight—these imbue the whole affair of fly fishing with a dramatic structure, like a novel. Emma's insult on Box Hill or Huck Finn's resolution to go to hell are but literary versions of a drifting fly. All are local and specific points at which something is on the verge of unfolding. In its details and techniques, fly fishing may be poetry, but the fact of the fly gives it the shape of narrative. (1994, 49)

Among the ironies of fly fishing, perhaps the most intriguing is the place of others in its activities. Fishing, like writing, is at heart a solitary activity, yet one that seems to demand, if it is to have any value beyond simple self-gratification, an audience. The great fishing experience—and all anglers, however occasional, have several of them—is worthless if it cannot be shared with others. Those others might only be friends and family, or they might be widespread readers of a major magazine, but the tale must be told. Fishing writing, done well, takes the reader into that magical moment of angling. At its best, it brings the reader into an unknown space within the angler, a space that, on its surface, might not seem worthy of consideration, but, under the direction of an expert guide opens into a world that is at once familiar and alien. The ultimate fruit of fishing and of its close relation, angling literature and stories, is not just the creation of a remarkable moment of time and space, but also the compulsion to relate those moments to others.

That compulsion, according to Bryn Hammond, is not the exclusive province of a few angling authors. What makes such writers as Lyons, Gierach, Leeson, and McGuane special is not that they see more than others but that they actually commit their visions to the page. Hammond suggests that there "isn't a fly fisherman alive who does not truly believe that he should keep a fishing diary. Yet few do. It is always a matter of starting one at the beginning of next season, yet that rarely happens. Most fishing diaries start off with literary enthusiasm; then dwindle after two or three lessening entries to a few scribbled hieroglyphics regarding the place or the catch: then nothing" (1994, 179).

As has been detailed above, fly fishing is an activity that is rich in relationship-building. The angler comes into relationship with rod and tackle, shore and stream, and, if all goes well, with the fish. The act of writing about fishing is a more abstract connection, by which the writer-angler reaches out with verbal flies and attempts to hook another human, yet just as the act of hooking the fish is often described as a way of discovering something about the angler, so, too, the act of writing is more efficient at reaching toward the self of the writer than toward the reader. Perhaps the ultimate abstraction in the range of relationships is the I-Thou relationship in which the "Thou" is the self. It seems that only in written expression does the angler's creation of a coherent self find completion. Extending Descartes, the angler might be quoted as saying, "I write, therefore I am." It is therefore fitting to consider the way fly fishing creates and refines the angler's relation to the text and therefore to the self.

While writing is a form of communication forging a link between author and audience, it is at the same time, and perhaps more importantly, a process by which the writer defines and delineates a self. Like fishing, writing places the author at midstream in the context of past and future with a hope of coming to know the now. Both arts place the actor in a space that exists between nature and humanity with a hope of knowing the self. This immediate knowledge is perhaps the best one can hope, a starting point from which to observe and explore the world genuinely. This is perhaps the knowledge that Eliot's narrator has glimpsed at the end of *The Waste Land* when he sits on the shore fishing, resolved to "at least set *my* lands in order" (emphasis mine).

The role of the North American fly angler is best expressed in the allegorical treatment offered by David James Duncan in *The River Why*. Gus

Orviston believed that he knew about fishing and about life, yet he discovered that he truly understood neither, a point punctuated by his snagging of the corpse while Gus was drifting downriver. Knowledge, whether of fishing or of language, is a more difficult thing than most would like to believe, but, as J. Hillis Miller advises, although "the truth about language may be a dark and troubling one, it is better to know that truth than to fool oneself or others" (1985, 113). Anglers are urged to cast into the future, hoping to make connection with others and, through that connection, to reach a better understanding of their irreducible selves, providing the foundation for true knowledge.

Works Cited

Auckley, Jim. 1994. "From Flippin' Sticks to Fly Rods." *Missouri Conservationist* (May): 8–11.

Baker, Sheridan. 1975. "Hemingway's Two-Hearted River." In *The Short Stories of Ernest Hemingway: Critical Essays,* ed. Jackson J. Benson. Durham, N.C.: Duke University Press.

Barclay, William. 1975. *The Gospel of John.* Vol. 1. Philadelphia: Westminster.

———. 1978. *The Gospel of Matthew.* Vol. 2. Philadelphia: Westminster.

Barich, Bill. 1990. "Frequent Fliers." In *The Fly Fisher's Reader,* ed. Leonard M. Wright Jr., 13–18. New York: Simon and Schuster.

Bentley, Gerald Eades, ed. 1958. *The Arte of Angling.* Princeton, N.J.: Princeton University Press.

Berners, Dame Juliana. 1963a. "Modernized Text of the Earliest Surviving Version of the *Treatise* (from the *Manuscript:* 1450)." In *The Origins of Angling* by John McDonald, 27–41. Garden City, N.Y.: Doubleday.

———.1963b. "Modernized Text of the First Printed Version of the *Treatise.*" In *The Origins of Angling* by John McDonald, 44–66. Garden City, N.Y.: Doubleday.

Bevan, Jonquil. 1993. Introduction to *The Compleat Angler* by Izaak Walton. London: Everyman.

Blackwood, Elsie M. 1968. *Many Rivers.* London: A. S. Barnes.

Blaisdell, Harold F. 1969. *The Philosophical Fisherman.* Boston: Houghton Mifflin.

Bode, Carl. 1977. Introduction to *The Portable Thoreau.* New York: Penguin.

Borgwordt, Cindy. 1993. "Philatelic Fish." *Missouri Conservationist* (January): 14–17.

Buber, Martin. 1958. *I and Thou.* 2d ed. Trans. Ronald Gregor Smith. New York: Macmillan.

Burton, Mallory. 1991a. "The Emerger." In *Uncommon Waters*, ed. Holly Morris, 11–14. Seattle: Seal.

———.1991b. "Mentors." In *Uncommon Waters*, ed. Holly Morris, 271–76. Seattle: Seal

———.1995. *Reading the Water: Stories and Essays of Flyfishing and Life*. Sandpoint, Idaho: Keokee.

Butler, Douglas R. 1992. "Norman Maclean's 'A River Runs through It': Word, Water, and Text." *Critique* 33: 263–73.

Camuto, Christopher. 1988. "Consciousness of Streams." *Sierra* (March/April): 48–51.

———. 1990. *A Fly Fisherman's Blue Ridge*. New York: Holt.

Chatham, Russell. 1978. "Angler's Afternoon." *Field and Stream* (March): 46ff.

———. 1990. "No Wind in the Willows." In *The Fly Fisher's Reader*, ed. Leonard M.Wright Jr., 195–204. New York: Simon and Schuster.

———, ed. 1988. *Silent Seasons*. Livingston, Mont.: Clark City Press.

Churchill, George B. 1924. "Miramichi Days." *Field and Stream* (August): 54–58.

Curtis, Jack. 1988. "Grandfather." In *Silent Seasons*, ed. Russell Chatham, 59–72. Livingston, Mont.: Clark City Press.

Davidson, Arnold E., and Cathy N. Davidson. 1987. "Decoding the Hemingway Hero in *The Sun Also Rises*." In *New Essays on* The Sun Also Rises, ed. Linda Wagner-Martin, 83–107. Cambridge: Cambridge University Press.

DeFalco, Joseph. 1963. *The Hero in Hemingway's Short Stories*. Pittsburgh: University of Pittsburgh Press.

Deloria, Vine. 1991. "Sacred Lands and Religious Freedom." *Native American Rights Fund Legal Review* (Summer): 1–6.

Devine, Robert S. 1995. "The Trouble With Dams." *Atlantic Monthly* (August): 64–74.

Duncan, David James. 1983. *The River Why*. New York: Bantam.

———.1995. *River Teeth*. New York: Doubleday.

Dunne, John William. 1924. *Sunshine and the Dry Fly*. London: A. and C. Black.

Edye, Huish. 1990. "The Mannerisms of Big Trout." In *The Fly Fisher's Reader*, ed. Leonard M.Wright Jr., 183–89. New York: Simon and Schuster.

Eliot, T. S. 1971. *Four Quartets*. San Diego: Harcourt Brace Jovanovich.

Emerson, Ralph Waldo. 1842. "Preliminary Note." *Dial* 3: 19.

Fenton, J. C. 1970. *The Gospel According to John*. Oxford: Oxford University Press.

Flora, Joseph M. 1982. *Hemingway's Nick Adams*. Baton Rouge: Louisiana State University Press.

Ford, Corey. 1990. "The Best-Loved Trout Stream of Them All." In *The Fly Fisher's Reader*, ed. Leonard M. Wright Jr., 226–38. New York: Simon and Schuster.

———. 1995. *Trout Tales and Other Angling Stories*. Comp. Laurie Morrow. Bozeman, Mont.: Wilderness Adventures Press.

Franson, Bob. 1993. "The Angler's Art." *Missouri Conservationist* (September): 27–30.

Frazer, Sir James George. 1959. *The New Golden Bough*. Ed. Theodor H. Gaster. New York: New American Library.

Gallagher, Tess. 1991. "Boat Ride." In *Uncommon Waters*, ed. Holly Morris, 23–28. Seattle: Seal.

Garner, Lewis-Ann. 1991. "One for the Glass Case." In *Uncommon Waters*, ed. Holly Morris, 149–54. Seattle: Seal.

Garrell, Martin H. 1993. "Anglers Always Dwell in the Past." *Sea Frontiers* (September/October): 18–19.

———. 1994. "Styles in Angling." *Sea Frontiers* (August): 16–17.

Gierach, John. 1990. *Sex, Death, and Fly-Fishing*. New York: Simon and Schuster.

———. 1991. *Where the Trout Are All as Long as Your Leg*. New York: Lyons and Burford.

Gordon, Theodore. 1990. "Jottings of a Fly-Fisher." In *The Fly Fisher's Reader*, ed. Leonard M. Wright Jr., 87–94. New York: Simon and Schuster.

Hackle, Sparse Grey. 1990. "The Father of the Fly Rod." In *The Fly Fisher's Reader*, ed. Leonard M. Wright Jr., 118–29. New York: Simon and Schuster.

Haig-Brown, Roderick [Langmere, 1908–1976]. 1975a. *Fisherman's Fall*. New York: Nick Lyons Books.

———. 1975b. *Fisherman's Spring*. New York: Nick Lyons Books.

———. 1975c. *Fisherman's Summer*. New York: Nick Lyons Books.

———. 1975d. *Fisherman's Winter*. New York: Nick Lyons Books.

———. 1981. *The Master and His Fish*. Ed. Valerie Haig-Brown. Seattle: University of Washington Press.

———. 1990. *Measure of the Year*. New York: Nick Lyons Books.

Hammond, Bryn. 1994. *Halcyon Days: The Nature of Trout Fishing and Fishermen*. Camden, Maine: Ragged Mountain.

Harrison, Jim. 1988. "A Sporting Life." In *Silent Seasons*, ed. Russell Chatham, 157–70. Livingston, Mont.: Clark City Press.

Haworth, John T. 1983. "Satisfaction Statements and the Study of Angling in the United Kingdom." *Leisure Sciences* 5: 181–96.

Hemingway, Ernest. 1925. *In Our Time*. New York: Boni and Liveright.

———. 1932. *Death in the Afternoon*. New York: Scribner.

———. 1952. *The Old Man and the Sea*. New York: Scribner.

———. 1964. *A Moveable Feast*. New York: Scribner.

———. 1970. *The Sun Also Rises*. New York: Scribner.

———. 1976. *Byline: Ernest Hemingway: Selected Articles and Dispatches of Four Decades*. New York: Scribner.

———. 1981. *Ernest Hemingway: Selected Letters*. Ed. Carlos Baker. New York: Scribner.

———. 1984. *Ernest Hemingway on Writing*. Ed. Larry W. Phillips. New York: Scribner.

———. 1990. "The Best Rainbow Trout Fishing." In *The Fly Fisher's Reader*, ed. Leonard M. Wright Jr., 205–8. New York: Simon and Schuster.

Hemingway, Jack. 1986. *Misadventures of a Fly Fisherman: My Life with and without Papa*. Dallas: Taylor Publishing.

Hemingway, Lorian. 1991. "The Young Woman and the Sea." In *Uncommon Waters*, ed. Holly Morris, 35–50. Seattle: Seal.

———. 1996. "Walk on Water for Me." In *The Gift of Trout*, ed. Ted Leeson, 37–48. New York: Lyons and Burford.

Henkin, Harmon. 1988. "New Breed." In *Silent Seasons*, ed. Russell Chatham, 105–17. Livingston, Mont.: Clark City Press.

Hersey, John. *Blues*. 1987. New York: Knopf.

Hesiod. 1973. *Works and Days*. Trans. Dorothea Wender. London: Penguin.

Hills, John Waller. 1990. "The Iron Blue." In *The Fly Fisher's Reader*, ed. Leonard M. Wright Jr., 36–41. New York: Simon and Schuster.

Hoover, Herbert. 1963. *Fishing for Fun and to Wash Your Soul*. Ed. William Nichols. New York: Random House.

Hope, Jack. 1984. "The Well-Lured Trout." *Science 84*.5: 160–67.

Hultkrantz, Ake. 1979. *The Religions of the American Indians*. Trans. Monica Setterwall. Berkeley: University of California Press.

Humphrey, William. 1978. *My Moby Dick*. Garden City, New York: Doubleday.

———. 1990. "The Spawning Run." In *The Fly Fisher's Reader*, ed. Leonard M. Wright Jr., 252–88. New York: Simon and Schuster.

Johnson, Phillip. 1986. "Learning the Language of a Stream." *National Wildlife* (August/September): 30–35.

Kruse, Mike. 1994. "A Comeback for Taneycomo Trout." *Missouri Conservationist* (March): 34.

Kuss, Mary S. 1991. "Jesus, Pete, It's a Woman Fly Fishing!" In *Uncommon Waters*, ed. Holly Morris, 59–69. Seattle: Seal.

La Branche, George M. L. 1951. *The Dry Fly and Fast Water,* and *The Salmon and the Dry Fly*. New York: Scribner.

Lawrence, H. Lea. 1992. *Prowling Papa's Waters: A Hemingway Odyssey*. Atlanta: Longstreet Press.

Leeson, Ted. 1994. *The Habit of Rivers: Reflections on Trout Streams and Fly Fishing*. New York: Lyons and Burford.

————, ed. 1996. *The Gift of Trout*. New York: Lyons and Burford.

Legler, Gretchen. 1996. "Fishergirl." In *A Different Angle,* ed. Holly Morris, 43–76. New York: Berkley.

Leonard, J. Edson. 1978. "The Metamorphosis of the Quill Gordon." *Field and Stream* (June): 49ff.

Lopez, Barry. 1989. *Crossing Open Ground*. New York: Vintage.

Low, Jim. 1994. "Trout Togetherness." *Missouri Conservationist* (February): 34.

Luce. A[rthur] A[ston, 1882–]. 1993. *Fishing and Thinking*. Camden, Maine: Ragged Mountain.

Lyons, Nick. 1977. *Bright Rivers*. Philadelphia: Lippincott.

————. 1989. *Confessions of a Fly Fishing Addict*. New York: Simon and Schuster.

————. 1992. *Spring Creek*. New York: Atlantic Monthly Press.

————. 1994. "On a Small Creek." *Fly Fisherman* (December): 95–96.

————. 1996. *A Flyfisher's World*. New York: Atlantic Monthly Press.

Maclean, Norman. 1976. *A River Runs through It and Other Stories*. Chicago: University of Chicago Press.

Macluin, T. D. 1981. "The Story-Teller." Part 3 of "Three Views of Haig-Brown." *Canadian Literature* 89: 181–83.

Markham, Gervase. 1927. *The Pleasures of Princes*. London: Cresset Press.

Marston, R. B. 1894. *Walton and Some Earlier Writers on Fish and Fishing*. London: Elliot Stack.

Martin, Calvin. 1978. *Keepers of the Game: Indian-Animal Relationships and the Fur Trade*. Berkeley: University of California Press.

McDonald, John. 1963. *The Origins of Angling*. Garden City, N.Y.: Doubleday.

McGuane, Thomas. 1988a. "Casting on a Sea of Memories." In *Silent Seasons,* ed. Russell Chatham, 13–20. Livingston, Mont.: Clark City Press.

————. 1988b. "The Longest Season." In *Silent Seasons,* ed. Russell Chatham, 3–12. Livingston, Mont.: Clark City Press.

———. 1988c. "Twilight on the Buffalo Paddock." In *Silent Seasons*, ed. Russell Chatham: 21–28. Livingston, Mont.: Clark City Press.

McLarney, William O. 1996. "Who Says They Don't Make Trout Streams Anymore?" In *The Gift of Trout*, ed. Ted Leeson, 161–74. New York: Lyons and Burford.

Miller, J. Hillis. 1985. "The Two Rhetorics: George Eliot's Bestiary." In *Writing and Reading Differently*, ed. G. Douglas Atkins and Michael L. Johnson. Lawrence: University Press of Kansas.

Montgomery, M. R. 1995. *Many Rivers to Cross: Of Good Running Water, Native Trout, and the Remains of Wilderness*. New York: Simon and Schuster.

Mooney, James. 1992. *James Mooney's History, Myths, and Sacred Formulas of the Cherokees*. Asheville, N.C.: Historical Images.

Moore, Kathleen Dean. 1995. *Riverwalking: Reflections on Moving Water*. San Diego: Harcourt Brace.

Morris, Holly, ed. 1991. *Uncommon Waters: Women Write about Fishing*. Seattle: Seal.

———. 1996. *A Different Angle: Fly Fishing Stories by Women*. New York: Berkley.

Norman, Geoffrey. 1987. "The Art of Trout Fishing." *National Wildlife* (April/May): 52–59.

Patterson, Neil. 1995. *Chalkstream Chronicle: Living Out a Flyfisher's Fantasy*. New York: Lyons and Burford.

Paul, Sherman. 1972. *The Shores of America: Thoreau's Inward Exploration*. Urbana: University of Illinois Press.

Perry, Bliss. 1927. *Pools and Ripples: Fishing Essays*. Boston: Little, Brown.

Quinnett, Paul. 1994. "Pavlov's Trout." *American Forests* (June): 44–47, 86.

Radcliffe, William. 1926. *Fishing from the Earliest Times*. London: John Murray.

Raines, Howell. 1994. *Fly Fishing Through the Midlife Crisis*. New York: Anchor.

Raymond, Steve. 1995. *The Year of the Angler*. Seattle: Sasquatch.

Read, S. E. 1981. "The Intellectual Fisherman." Part 1 of "Three Views of Haig-Brown." *Canadian Literature* 89: 178–82.

Reynolds, Michael S. 1988. The Sun Also Rises: *A Novel of the Twenties*. Boston: Twayne.

Robson, John M. 1990. "The Physics of Fly Casting." *American Journal of Physics* 58: 234–40.

Roosevelt, Theodore. 1990. *Outdoor Pastimes of an American Hunter*. Harrisburg, Pa.: Stackpole Books.

Sahrhage, Dietrich, and Johannes Lundbeck. 1992. *A History of Fishing*. Berlin: Springer Verlag.

Sandor, Marjorie. 1996. "The Noviate's Tale." In *The Gift of Trout*, ed. Ted Leeson, 49–54. New York: Lyons and Burford.

Schreiber, Le Anne. 1990. *Midstream: A Mother's Death and a Daughter's Renewal.* New York: Viking.

———."The Long Light." 1991. In *Uncommon Waters*, ed. Holly Morris, 3–9. Seattle: Seal.

Smith, Janet Adam. 1965. *John Buchan: A Biography.* London: Rupert Hart-Davis.

Smith, Julian. 1970–71. "Hemingway and the Thing Left Out." *Journal of Modern Literature* 1: 169–72.

Sojka, Gregory S. 1985. *Ernest Hemingway: The Angler as Artist.* New York: Peter Lang.

Spolek, Graig A. 1986. "The Mechanics of Flycasting: The Flyline." *American Journal of Physics* 54: 832–36.

Stoltzfus, Ben. 1991. *"The Old Man and the Sea*: A Lacanian Reading." In *Hemingway: Essays of Reassessment*, ed. Frank Scafella. New York: Oxford University Press.

Stowell, Robert F. 1970. *A Thoreau Gazetteer.* Ed. William L. Howarth. Princeton, N.J.: Princeton University Press.

Sutherland, Lin. 1996. "A River Ran Over Me." In *A Different Angle*, ed. Holly Morris, 3–11. New York: Berkley.

Thoreau, Henry David. 1977a. *Walden. The Portable Thoreau*, ed. Carl Bode, 258–572. Rev. ed. New York: Penguin.

———. 1977b. *A Week on the Concord and Merrimack Rivers.* In *The Portable Thoreau*, ed. Carl Bode, 138–227. Rev. ed. New York: Penguin.

Three Books on Fishing. 1962. Gainesville, Florida: Scholars' Facsimiles and Reprints.

Tirana, Turhan. 1996. *Fly Fishing: A Life in Mid-Stream.* New York: Kensington Books.

Traver, Robert. 1989. *Trout Madness.* New York: Simon and Schuster.

Travler, Ailm. 1991. "Fly Fishing Folly." In *Uncommon Waters*, ed. Holly Morris, 207–12. Seattle: Seal.

Tryon, Chuck, and Sharon Tryon. 1992. *Fly Fishing for Trout in Missouri.* Rolla, Mo.: Ozark Mountain Fly Fishers.

Turner, Spence. 1994. "The Four Seasons of Lake Taneycomo." *Missouri Conservationist* (December): 4–7.

Underhill, Evelyn. 1990. *Mysticism.* New York: Image.

United States Bureau of the Census. 1994. *Statistical Abstract of the United States: 1994.* 114th ed. Washington: U.S. Bureau of the Census.

Von Kienbusch, Carl Otto. 1958. Introduction to *The Arte of Angling*. Princeton, N.J.: Princeton University Press.

Walton, Izaak. 1993. *The Compleat Angler, or, The Contemplative Man's Recreation*. London: Everyman.

Weston, Jessie L. 1993. *From Ritual to Romance*. Princeton, N.J.: Princeton University Press.

Woodcock, George. 1981. "The Naturalist." Part 2 of "Three Views of Haig-Brown." *Canadian Literature* 89: 180–81.

———. 1990. "Introduction to Haig-Brown, Roderick." In *Measure of the Year* by Roderick Haig-Brown. New York: Nick Lyons Books.

Wright, Leonard M., Jr., ed. 1990. *The Fly Fisher's Reader*. New York: Simon and Schuster.

Wulff, Joan Salvato. 1991. "Where I Want to Be." In *Uncommon Waters*, ed. Holly Morris, 93–95. Seattle: Seal.

Yeats, William Butler. 1962. *Selected Poems and Three Plays*. Ed. M. L. Rosenthal. New York: Macmillan.

Index